Scripting a Sermon

Scripting a Sermon

Using the Wisdom of Filmmaking
for Impactful Preaching

SHAUNA HANNAN
AND
GAEL CHANDLER

WESTMINSTER
JOHN KNOX PRESS
LOUISVILLE · KENTUCKY

First edition
Published by Westminster John Knox Press
Louisville, Kentucky

24 25 26 27 28 29 30 31 32 33—10 9 8 7 6 5 4 3 2 1

Book design by Drew Stevens
Cover design by Lisa Buckley Design

Library of Congress Cataloging-in-Publication Data

Names: Hannan, Shauna. (Shauna Kay), author. | Chandler, Gael, 1951– author.
Title: Scripting a sermon : using the wisdom of filmmaking for impactful preaching / Shauna Hannan and Gael Chandler.
Description: First edition. | Louisville, Kentucky : Westminster John Knox Press, [2024] | Series: Preaching and | Includes bibliographical references and index. | Summary: "Approaches common challenges for crafting sermons looking toward the essential components of filmmaking to help preachers create more potent sermons"—Provided by publisher.
Identifiers: LCCN 2024035231 (print) | LCCN 2024035232 (ebook) | ISBN 9780664268169 (paperback) | ISBN 9781646984077 (ebook)
Subjects: LCSH: Motion pictures—Homiletical use. | Motion pictures—Religious aspects—Christianity. | Preaching.
Classification: LCC BV4235.M68 H36 2024 (print) | LCC BV4235.M68 (ebook) | DDC 251/.01—dc23/eng/20240906
LC record available at https://lccn.loc.gov/2024035231
LC ebook record available at https://lccn.loc.gov/2024035232

Most Westminster John Knox Press books are available at special quantity discounts when purchased in bulk by corporations, organizations, and special-interest groups. For more information, please email SpecialSales@wjkbooks.com.

To the late Dean Olson, Director of Concordia College Television Center, Moorhead, Minnesota.
—*Shauna Hannan*

To the late Michael Wiese, producer-director-author-publisher, who said, "Write your books for where you want them to take you." While I never know where they will take me, this one continues to be an unexpected, rich, ever-unfolding journey.
—*Gael Chandler*

Contents

Preface to the "Preaching and . . ." Series

Preachers are not just preachers. When they step into the pulpit they are also theologians, storytellers, biblical teachers, pastors, historians, psychologists, entertainers, prophets, anthropologists, leaders, political scientists, popular culture commentators, ethicists, philosophers, scientists, and so much more. It is not that they are expected to be masters of homiletics and jacks of all other trades. Instead it is that when preachers strive to bring God's good news to bear on the whole of human existence, a lot is required to connect the two in existentially appropriate and meaningful ways.

The Perkins Center for Preaching Excellence (PCPE), directed by Alyce M. McKenzie, has partnered with Westminster John Knox Press to create a book series that contributes to that work in a new way. While homiletical scholarship has long drawn on the full range of biblical and theological disciplines as well as a variety of philosophical and rhetorical disciplines, this series attempts to push the interdisciplinary dialogue in new ways. For each volume, the PCPE brings together as coauthors two scholars—a homiletician and an expert from another, nontheological field to bring that field into conversation with homiletics in a way that offers both new insights into preaching as a task and vocation and new strategies for the practical elements of sermon preparation and delivery.

The first two volumes brought preaching into conversation with advertising and humor studies. In this third volume, preachers are given the chance to examine their homiletical practices through the diverse lenses of filmmaking. What preacher has not left a movie or turned off a television and thought, "I wish I could preach with that kind of effect"? Shauna Hannan and Gael Chandler help us bridge that gap.

O. Wesley Allen Jr.
Series Editor

Introduction

The film and television industry has exploded in popularity as shows are available on the big screen, home theater systems, and even cell phones. It's as if everyone is wired for the screen. This reason alone makes it worth a preacher's time to become adept at the language of film. Increasingly, people have more cinematic literacy than biblical literacy. In their book *Deep Focus*, Robert K. Johnston, Craig Detweiler, and Kutter Callaway confirm the cultural importance of films: "The cinema has become an important means of cultural communication, a contemporary language in need of understanding and explication. . . . Some even believe that cinema studies is positioned to become the new MBA, a means of general preparation for careers in fields as diverse as law and the military."[1] Although multimedia literacy is not one of the accreditation standards for theological schools (yet!), add theological studies to these diverse fields.

For many, visual images (whether still or moving) have replaced text as the central tool of communication. This substitution challenges theology's centrality of the Word (text) and revives a long-standing love/hate relationship between the pious and images. The obstacles are especially palpable for an oral/aural ecclesial practice like preaching. After all, faith comes through hearing (Rom. 10:17), not seeing,

---

1. Robert K. Johnston, Craig Detweiler, and Kutter Callaway, *Deep Focus: Film and Theology in Dialogue* (Grand Rapids: Baker Academic Press, 2019), 11.

right? Despite such challenges, the Reformation spirit asks theologians to embrace new means of communicating the gospel. Might *cinematic literacy* be today's printing press?[2]

As seminary education continues to follow the higher education trend toward online teaching and learning, instructors recognize the need to enhance their multimedia literacy. Minimally, it is important to note that many of our students are already literate in the contemporary language of cinema. Churches, too, have been dabbling in the use of images, from iconography to screens in the sanctuary. The COVID-19 pandemic thrust preachers and other church leaders onto the virtual screen scene in new ways, and many have continued an online presence even when it was safe to gather in person again. Clearly the need for multimedia literacy is not going away. Again, as the authors of *Deep Focus* put it, "Movies serve not simply as a commodity but as a primary storytelling medium of the twenty-first century, interpreting reality for us, providing us with a common language, and acting as a type of cultural glue."[3]

The aim of this book is to boost preachers' cinematic literacy—which we are defining as the ability to decipher and interpret the content and language of films as told with pictures and sounds via acting, directing, cinematography, and editing—in order to seek convergences between filmmaking and homiletics for the purposes of enlivening the preached word, communicating the gospel, and impacting hearers and our world. We reference many films and film scenes and encourage you to watch them. They are readily available on disk or online (links are not provided because they are subject to changes or vanishing).

DIFFERENCES AND SIMILARITIES

To be sure, the differences between the two crafts are evident. One is primarily oral/aural and the other visual. One is generally live, the other preproduced. One is explicitly located within a religious/spiritual setting in the present, and the other can be located anywhere at any time. Preaching requires a product each week, if not multiple products within a week, and films routinely take years to produce. Whereas films are often entirely fabricated, preaching is expected to be "based on true events."

Despite numerous differences between the two fields, there are enough similarities that preachers have much to learn from filmmakers.

2. Terms that are in the "Key Filmmaking Terms" glossary are italicized on first use.
3. Johnston, Detweiler, and Callaway, *Deep Focus*, 10.

This book will show that both professions seek to impact others and the world and both do so by paying attention to the reactions and subsequent actions of the "audience." Filmmakers and preachers alike use techniques that can be traditional or unconventional. Their work is served by being collaborative and interactive. Both crafts require a balance of perspiration and inspiration, the "mundane and the magical," you might say. The latter highlights the mystery of the process, which may produce something different (better or worse) than the hoped-for or visualized results. Even so, the intentionality of the filmmaker offers food for thought for preachers, which the book's chapters will highlight.

THE SCOPE OF THE BOOK

Timothy Cargal notes that "several writers have discussed the cultural prominence and importance of film by describing it as a '*lingua franca*' or '"cultural currency" in which discussions about life and death (and life and depth) issues are conducted.'"[4] We hope that preachers might tap into this lingua franca in order to assist churchgoers in discussions about life and death and life and depth (!) issues.

Religion and film have been connected ever since the first films in the late nineteenth century, such as *The Horitz Passion Play* (1897) and *Passion Play of Oberammergau* (1898). Before the First World War, more than seventy films based on biblical themes were shot. Even so, at times religion has opposed film by forbidding churchgoers from going to cinemas and banning certain movies, as exemplified by the Production Code and the Roman Catholic Church's Legion of Decency developed in the 1930s.[5] Some religious organizations have continued the obstruction attempts with an eight-year boycott of Disney

---

4. Timothy B. Cargal, *Hearing a Film, Seeing a Sermon: Preaching and Popular Movies* (Louisville, KY: Westminster John Knox Press, 2007), 3. Cargal cites Robert K. Johnston, *Reel Spirituality: Theology and Film in Dialogue* (Grand Rapids: Baker Academic, 2000); Clive Marsh and Gaye Ortiz, eds., *Explorations in Theology and Film* (Oxford: Blackwell, 1997); and Craig Detweiler and Barry Taylor, *A Matrix of Meanings: Finding God in Pop Culture* (Grand Rapids: Baker Academic, 2003).

5. A Hollywood motion picture standard instituted in 1934 and enforced until 1968, the Hays Code, as it was popularly known, prohibited profanity, nudity, drug use, sex, miscegenation, ridicule of the clergy, childbirth, and more in movies and was promoted by Christian sects.

(1997–2005) and current cries to defund the company along with castigating certain movies and Hollywood in general. More recently, some have demonized Oscar-nominated *Barbie* (2023) for its gender roles and transgender characters, calling for a boycott, and they presumably wouldn't have warmed up to director-cowriter Greta Gerwig's comments in a *Vox* interview, "Barbie was invented first. Ken was invented after Barbie to burnish Barbie's position in our eyes and in the world. That kind of creation myth is the opposite of the creation myth in Genesis."[6]

All the while, theologians have mined films for biblical themes and filmmakers have sought out theologians as conversation partners when incorporating theological themes into their films. Many books address these concerns. This book is different, however. It focuses on craft and asks what preachers can learn from filmmakers in order to apply cinematic literacy to their homiletical craft.

Each chapter identifies common challenges for crafting sermons and then presents essential components of filmmaking that preachers might employ for more effective preaching. Throughout the book we draw from a variety of filmmaking genres, such as drama, comedy, documentary, and horror, since we believe that every film genre can be fodder for preachers as they develop their craft. Even more, multiple filmmaking formats (e.g., feature film, short film, television series) are useful for increasing one's cinematic literacy for the purpose of sermonic impact.

Coming Attractions

Chapter 1, "Begin with the End: Shooting for Impact." Sermons that are detached from the realities of people's lives have little impact on belief and behavior. This chapter identifies the techniques filmmakers use to focus on their audience and to create impact and translates them into suitable techniques for preachers.

---

6. Alissa Wilkinson, "In the Beginning, There Was Barbie: Turns Out Greta Gerwig's Barbie Movie Is a Biblical Metaphor after All," *Vox*, July 20, 2023, www .vox.com/culture/23800753/barbie-review-bible-eden. See also Jennifer Sandlin, "Evangelicals Rail against Barbie, Demand Americans Not Take Children to See Film," boingboing, July 20, 2023, https://boingboing.net/2023/07/20/evangelicals -rail-against-barbie-demand-americans-not-take-children-to-see-film.html.

Chapter 2, "Cast and Crew: Collaborating for Impact." Sermons that represent only one person's work and viewpoint fail to equip people to fulfill their baptismal call to proclaim. This chapter demystifies how film directors, cast, and crew work together to create and deliver a show. It challenges preachers to move beyond operating as solo artists in order to empower others to become part of a sermon's cast and crew.

Chapter 3, "Fade In: Creating the Opening." Sermon openings that are disconnected from the rest of the sermon or from the biblical pericope neglect to set in motion the sermon's theme, tone, and hoped-for outcome. The chapter discusses how filmmakers create opening scenes that set up the rest of the film and provides concrete recommendations for making the first minutes of a sermon more impactful.

Chapter 4, "Scenes, Beats, and Pacing: The Building Blocks." Sermons, like films, can try to do too much or go in too many directions with too many characters, losing their audience or leaving them confused. The chapter covers how filmmakers construct scenes and script narratives that flow at an understandable, believable rate.

Chapter 5, "Cut by Cut: Editing for Story and Audience." Preachers should think like film editors who stand in for the audience and act as the final writer by pacing the story, removing shots and scenes that do not forward the action, and asking with every cut, What does the audience need now? What do they need to know with each sentence, paragraph, story, and claim?

Chapter 6, "Fade Out: Creating the Closing." Sermons often contain too many endings or finish too abruptly. Preachers might wonder how to "land the plane." This chapter highlights the ways films reach their final fade-out and presents preachers with choices for making a sermon's closing most effective.

Chapter 7, "Outtakes." This short closing chapter builds on the rest, offering final recommendations and challenges, such as looking at preaching and artificial intelligence (AI), considering a sermon's sound track, and creating a trailer (preview) of a sermon.

1

Begin with the End: Shooting for Impact

Movies change us. Sermons change us too. We hope. In this time of increasing cinematic literacy, not only have we developed the sense that films are supposed to affect us but we also have the capacity to identify a film's impact on us beyond "I liked it" or "I didn't like it." Have you ever wondered why so many people share with others a film's impact on them but many (if not most) worshipers rarely talk with one another about their worship experience, especially the Sunday sermon? Imagine if churchgoers were impacted by a sermon and could share their experience beyond "I liked it" or "I didn't like it." Increasing such homiletical literacy begins with the practices of preachers themselves, which is why this chapter focuses on how preachers might achieve their desired impact as effectively as filmmakers do by doing what filmmakers do.

FILMMAKERS AND STORY

Identifying and Achieving Desired Impact

Where Filmmakers Start

Simply put, filmmakers start with the story they want to tell. This story can spring from a newspaper article, someone or something in the film-maker's life, a current or historical event or person, or a thread on social media. It can be "based on true events" or adapted from a play, novel, video game, or other creative entity. A story can also spring entirely from the creator's imagination, catalyzed by research, stream-of-conscious freewriting, *blue skying* (freewriting with others in a writer's room), and always by just plain putting pen to paper or keyboard to computer. The setting can be the past, present, or future as the story conveys an era, a life, an event, a philosophy, and much more.

Part of conceiving a show involves deciding how the story will best be told. Will it work better as a *documentary* or fiction? Should it be a short film, a feature, a TV series?[1] If fiction, what genre fits best? Some of the most impactful films have had little or no planning at all. Most people witnessed the impact of the video of George Floyd's murder, the news coverage of the gallant end of Serena Williams's decades-long career, and the televised US House Select Committee hearings about January 6. In these examples, filmmakers did not plan, they just captured. Normally, however, creating a story for a film involves months, if not years, of research and planning, inspiration, and perspiration until the film is exhibited and begins to impact viewers.

Reading the Audience

Filmmakers achieve maximum impact by paying careful attention to their potential audience from conception to delivery as they develop and present the story they want to tell. Simone Bartesaghi relates the director's process in his book *The Director's Six Senses:*

> We tell our stories by selecting words that our audience can understand. We try very hard to make sure that the story that begins in our mind will eventually become the same story in our audience's mind. . . . When the movie is watched by the audience, it's experienced again piece by piece, shot by shot, sound by sound, and it's important that the pieces of the puzzle are going to be put together with the same meaning by the audience.[2]

---

1. A feature has an ideal running time of ninety minutes; a TV show has a set, contracted time ranging from twenty-five to sixty minutes. A video might have no required length and be only minutes long (such as a music video) or last for seconds, as viral videos have repeatedly demonstrated. To summarize, duration depends on format and exhibition requirements.

2. Simone Bartesaghi, *The Director's Six Senses: An Innovative Approach to Developing Your Filmmaking Skills* (Studio City, CA: Michael Wiese Productions, 2016), xi–xii.

Underlying every decision a filmmaker makes about the story is a desire for and commitment to the film impacting the audience. Starting with the scriptwriter, filmmakers consider who their audience will be. While seeking as wide a viewership as possible, they will also target specific audiences, such as tweens, LGBTQIA+ people, and the global majority by their choice of subject matter, characters, actors, and genre. As one author puts it, "The filmmaker organizes shots, camera movement, editing, and music to elicit certain reactions so that viewers will respond right on cue precisely as intended."[3] Once filmmakers dream up the story, they need to be able to describe it quickly and clearly to potential buyers, collaborators, and viewers. Enter the *logline*.

Cinematic Loglines

Also referred to as a *one-liner*, a logline is a succinct sentence (sometimes two) that dynamically communicates what the movie or TV series is about. The logline is the elevator pitch, a high-concept summary of the screenplay, which should contain the opposing forces—protagonist and antagonist—and the conflict, what is at stake. Originally a nautical term, "logline" came into use in early Hollywood when the burgeoning studios began keeping logbooks with short summaries of the hundreds of scripts they owned. Here's a sample logline: A wealthy old woman remembers a love affair she had as a young woman on an ill-fated luxury liner (*Titanic*). If the movie is a documentary, the logline must show what the protagonist is up against, such as exposing a corporation's malfeasance, discovering a family secret, or revisiting a time in history with new research. For instance, the logline for *My Octopus Teacher* might be this: a divorced cinematographer dives deep into the ocean to befriend an octopus while seeking reconnection with his son.

How do filmmakers use a logline? Primarily, it's deployed by those who pitch the project—screenwriter, director, and producer—to secure funds or get the show produced by a studio or production company. People involved in *production* (filming) and *postproduction* (editing) will use their own words to describe the show to friends and family and be unaware of the logline. The logline may be refined as the show changes during script development and following *final cut* when it becomes part of the marketing campaign. The superpower of the logline throughout

---

3. William D. Romanowski, *Cinematic Faith: A Christian Perspective on Movies and Meaning* (Grand Rapids: Baker, 2019), 55.

the filmmaking process and during exhibition is to summarize the story and sell people on the show.

Film Genre and Impact

In developing the story, a filmmaker will determine not just *what* the story is about and *who* the intended audience is, but also *how* to tell it most faithfully and truthfully. Will it best be told as a drama? A thriller? A horror film? It is fitting that the film *mother!* (2017), with its biblical and allegorical elements of the contemporary plight of Mother Earth, is a psychological horror movie. Under what circumstances might a comedy work better than a documentary to illuminate a controversial or complex set of political truths? *Tootsie* (1982) aimed to portray life for aspiring actresses via its cross-dressing male lead character. Consider also the satirical comedy *Don't Look Up* (2021), an allegory for what could happen if we ignore our changing climate. Or would the science fiction genre be more fitting, as demonstrated in the dystopian *Snowpiercer* (2013), which skewered capitalism by focusing on a nonstop train with sealed cars segregated by social class that relentlessly circles the earth?

Films can amuse, illuminate, inform, motivate, manipulate, propagandize, frighten, and give catharsis. Each genre can and does do much more. Take, for example, documentaries. In their book *Producing with Passion*, Dorothy Fadiman and Tony Levelle note, "When you make a documentary, you hold the potential to open people's eyes and take them beyond their usual way of seeing the world."[4] Don Schwartz, film critic and regular contributor to the magazine *cineSOURCE*, suggests that choosing to see documentary films is like choosing the "red pill" from *The Matrix* (1999), thereby waking the person up—"giving him the opportunity to escape." He writes,

> It is the provocative films—on socio-political-economic injustice, on histories ignored, on our destruction of the world—that challenge our dearly-held beliefs and values. Documentary filmmakers are liberators; they offer the Red Pill. . . . Yes, the Red Pill tastes bitter; it can be deeply disturbing, demoralizing. Its side effects include nausea and vomiting as we release the phantasies

4. Dorothy Fadiman and Tony Levelle, *Producing with Passion: Making Films That Change the World* (Studio City, CA: Michael Wiese Productions, 2008), xiv.

[*sic*] we've engorged. Or, we may choose to remain "comfortably numb."[5]

In short, filmmakers want to create something that makes an audience feel something. Even more, they want something to happen.

How to Gauge Actual Impact

In the end, filmmakers learn the impact of their films from box office sales. However, well in advance of a film's release, they gauge impact by hosting prerelease screenings where they solicit viewers' oral and written feedback on the show's story, characters, plot, and theme along with its level of engagement and other criteria. During production and postproduction, filmmakers solicit input from colleagues and coworkers: screenwriter from writing groups, director from actors, cinematographer, editor, and producers. Filmmakers have a clue how their work will impact their audience. Still, as much as Hollywood moguls deem it the film "business," there are no infallible tools for predicting box office. A sure thing can flop, an independent movie can become a hit, a critics' darling can draw low returns, an art film can achieve a cult following.

Beyond the box office, there are other measures for how a film impacts an audience. One such indicator emerged in the 1980s. Created by comic artist and graphic novelist Alison Bechdel, the *Bechdel Test* measures the representation of women in movies and fiction.[6] To pass the test, a film must have at least two featured women who talk to each other about something other than a man. This informal analysis has been used to evaluate movies and TV shows and correlate them with box office returns. Research studies have consistently documented that films that pass the test perform better financially. Journalists Versha Sharma and Hanna Sender ran the Bechdel Test on the fifty top-grossing movies of 2013 and concluded, "The grand total domestic box office number for the movies that passed [the test] is significantly higher than the domestic box office total for the movies that didn't. We're

5. Don Schwartz, *Telling Their Own Stories: Conversations with Documentary Filmmakers* (Berkeley, CA: Don Schwartz, 2013), 2.

6. Bechdel's graphic memoir *Fun Home* morphed into a Broadway musical and won a Tony in 2015 and many other awards.

talking billions."[7] The Bechdel Test has fostered other tests, notably the Vito Russo Test for LGBTQIA+ portrayal, an Orthodox Jew test, and a test that examines characters with questions such as "Are there two named characters of color? Do they have dialogue that doesn't involve comforting or supporting a white person?"

In the final analysis, the impact on lives may add up to far more than box office receipts. Jeff Skoll, first president of eBay, chair of Participant Media, and executive producer of *An Inconvenient Truth* (2006), stated, "One metric of success that we use is whether more good comes from the film than just putting the money directly to work in a non-profit organization involved in the same issue. . . . We will take risks on projects where we think we might lose money, because we hope that the good that comes from that outweighs the risk. It's a different kind of philanthropy."[8]

Film Impact Teams

No filmmakers work more tirelessly toward a desired impact than documentary filmmakers. They rely on crowdsourcing and grants, partnering with individuals, not-for-profits, nongovernmental organizations (NGOs), and corporations not only for funds but also for spreading the word so that the film will reach its audience and achieve its desired impact. While social media, influencers, and reporters (print and online) are critical, documentary filmmakers have begun to put together "impact teams" to determine how films change hearts and minds and motivate their viewers to take action.[9] In addition to filmmakers and marketers, the impact team can be composed of consultants from other walks of life, including statisticians, nonprofit personnel, journalists, government employees, and social activists.

In the last decade, this desire for impact has advanced to a new level with the inception of a new filmmaking role, the "impact producer," who

7. Versa Sharma and Hanna Sender, "Hollywood Movies with Strong Female Roles Make More Money," *Vocativ,* January 2, 2014, quoted in Alanna Vagianos, "This Graph Proves That Everyone Loses When Hollywood Is Sexist," *Huffington Post,* January 3, 2014, https://www.huffpost.com/entry/hollywood-sexist-bechdel_test_vocativ_n_4536277.

8. *San Jose Mercury News* interview with Jeff Skoll by Bruce Newman, October 2005, quoted in "Beyond the Box Office: New Documentary Valuations," Channel 4 BRITDOC Foundation, May 2011, https://impactguide.org/static/library/AnInconvenientTruth_BeyondTheBoxOffice.pdf, 4.

9. Britdoc.org/Impact, "Meet the Impact Producer," *The Impact Field Guide and Toolkit: From Art to Impact,* https://impactguide.org/.

is responsible "for maximizing a film's potential for social change."[10] The impact producer and their team track trailer views, website traffic, audience and email list numbers, critics' responses, organizations partnered or worked with, Facebook likes, community screenings, theatrical and broadcast runs, festivals, and awards. *The Age of Stupid,* a 2009 UK film tackling climate change, allowed "anyone anywhere" to organize a film screening.[11] The impact team documented the results in their case study of *The Age of Stupid,* writing, "Crucially, the organiser [of the film screening] keeps any profits for themselves or their campaign. This empowers and engages audiences before they have even seen the film because, in a sense, it hands the film and its issues directly back to the audience."[12] The team concluded that "the impact of this film built on the awareness of the issues and saw not just individuals but corporations and governments commit to, and exceed, a 10% cut in their emissions."[13]

With audience participation in mind, the company Imagine Impact (launched in 2018 by Brian Grazer, Ron Howard, and Tyler Mitchell) created an "open submission process" in order to

> identify and develop feature film ideas in four specific genres over the next year that they will then bring to Netflix. . . . Imagine Impact was launched . . . as a means of accelerating and democratizing the script development process by attempting to remove bias from the submission process, allowing the writer's voice to speak for itself and the most viable projects to move forward, regardless of the applicant's location, demographic, or representation status.[14]

---

10. Impact producers are now listed on film credits. See https://impact-guide.org/impact-in-action/the-role-of-film-teams/ and Jackson DeMos, "Research Study Finds That a Film Can Have a Measurable Impact on Audience Behavior," USC Annenberg School for Communication and Journalism, updated May 3, 2023, https://annenberg.usc.edu/news/centers/research-study-finds-film-can-have-measurable-impact-audience-behavior.

11. Britdoc.org/Impact, "*The Age of Stupid* Case Study," The Impact Field Guide and Toolkit, https://impactguide.org/static/library/AgeOfStupid.pdf, 4.

12. "*Age of Stupid* Case Study," 4.

13. "*Age of Stupid* Case Study," 7.

14. Dave McNary, "Netflix Teams with Ron Howard and Brian Grazer's Imagine Impact to Develop Films from Rising Filmmakers," *Variety,* June 17, 2020, https://variety.com/2020/film/news/netflix-ron-howard-brian-grazer-imagine-1234637665/.

These kinds of entrepreneurial advances in the film industry highlight increased attention on audience impact even when films are hatched with an eye to ratings and the box office. It is fair to say that in raising awareness about a particular film, the impact team sometimes shapes the film itself. Filmmakers also benefit personally from focusing on impact in ways that range from respect to popularity and increased opportunities to make the kinds of films they are passionate about.

PREACHERS AND STORY

Identifying and Achieving Desired Impact

While preachers do not have the time or budget to engage in market research as filmmakers do, they stand to benefit by focusing on impact. There are a variety of manageable practices to glean from the filmmaking industry regarding how to impact audiences and to gauge the actual impact, for example, being clear about and refining the story being told, paying particular attention to the audience's needs, arranging prerelease "screenings," focusing on the "how" as well as the "what," and following up with hearers.

Where Preachers Start

Preachers begin with a story as well—the biblical story. Take a moment to identify how you might encapsulate God's story by filling in the blank:

The biblical story is about _____

_____

_____.

Taking a cue from the film industry's use of the logline—the high-concept summary—this statement should contain the opposing forces (protagonist and antagonist), the conflict, and what is at stake. For instance, one might say the biblical story is about how a divine being loves its creation so much that it becomes human both to understand the injustices experienced by the beloved creation and to challenge and overcome the oppressive systems that instigate those injustices.

The task then focuses on the question of how one might bring this grand narrative to life in the here and now, wherever and whenever that might be. Whereas literature's aim is to turn blood into ink, à la T. S. Eliot, preaching's aim is to turn ink (i.e., the written biblical text) into blood.[15] Preaching intends to bring the sacred text, God's story, to life. Christians have taken up this challenge in the pulpit ever since Jesus's death and resurrection.[16] In so doing, preaching focuses not necessarily on the grand narrative for each occasion but on the numerous individual stories that make up that grand narrative, be they about an event, an experience, a character, or a scene. The key for preachers is being clear about and staying focused on the story they're telling.

As noted in the introduction, the first film that attempts to tell the biblical story was produced fewer than two decades after the first motion picture. That film, *The Horitz Passion Play* (1897), was followed in 1898 by the eleven-minute film *La Passion*, by the Lumière brothers.[17] Hundreds of films on biblical stories have followed.[18] None of them attempted to tell the whole biblical story. They could not have done so because the story is far too broad, too exhaustive; it defies

15. Charles Bartow flips T. S. Eliot's claim. Bartow, *God's Human Speech: A Practical Theology of Proclamation* (Grand Rapids: Wm. B. Eerdmans Publishing Co., 1997), 43.

16. Recall what might be considered one of the first Christian sermons, as recounted in the Gospel of John. While weeping after seeing that the tomb where the crucified Jesus has been laid is empty, Mary Magdalene encounters someone who she thinks is the gardener. After a brief dialogue, she recognizes the person to be Jesus, who is alive. "Mary Magdalene went and announced to the disciples, 'I have seen the Lord,' and she told them that he had said these things to her" (John 20:18, NRSVue). That one line, "I have seen the Lord," is a sermon in the form of personal testimony, a timeless and effective form of preaching. From that first proclamation of Jesus's resurrection through today, preachers across the globe have been figuring out how to tell that story.

17. John Sanidopoulos, "Movie Review: The Passion (1898)," *Honey and Hemlock* (blog), March 3, 2020, http://www.honeyandhemlock.com/2020/03/movie-review-passion-1898.html. For an interesting view into films based on the Bible, visit the collection of biblical movie posters at https://www.dspt.edu/biblical-movie-poster-collection.

18. Films focused explicitly on religious themes are not the only films from which preachers can gain insight. As noted in the introduction, this book discusses a wide variety of film themes, most commonly those that do not focus solely on telling the biblical story.

being crammed into a fifteen-minute monologue, a short film, or even a ninety-minute film. Even filmmakers of the "greatest story ever told" tell the stories within the story. They choose a particular perspective from which to tell the story, highlighting specific characters, topics, plotlines, and genres and downplaying others as variously as sermons do. The opportunity for preachers, therefore, is to learn how filmmakers tell the story within a story effectively and adopt practices and techniques for preaching the biblical story insofar as they are appropriate and applicable; that is, insofar as they will impact a particular set of hearers in a manner fitting of God's good news.

Reading the Audience

Just as filmmakers benefit from considering their hoped-for audiences in the *development* and *preproduction* phases before *shooting* the show, so, too, might preachers pay attention to the particularities of their hearers even before they begin to craft their sermons. While the practices may not be exactly the same, the intention to impact the audience is. Intentional small steps go a long way when preachers "read their audience."

For starters, we recommend that preachers spend time (even if only fifteen to twenty minutes) at the beginning of their sermon-crafting process replying to these prompts: What is going on in the world? in the church? in your congregation? with certain individuals? with you? Addressing these and other relevant questions allows preachers to tap into the status quo and their people's lives from the start. Even though pastors accompany their congregation members as they live their lives, reflecting through writing can bring up some things that would otherwise be assumed or forgotten. Preachers might also make it a habit to ask two or three (or more) people these same questions for each sermon. Congregants will appreciate being asked.

Such preaching practices are acts of pastoral care both as a way to begin conversation with hearers and because they respect the particularities of others' experience by not making assumptions. In her book *Decolonizing Preaching*, Sarah Travis suggests that preachers "can only speak on behalf of others if they are in conversation with them. . . . Preachers cannot escape the problem of representing others, yet can strive to be as accurate as possible and clear that whenever we speak about others in our sermons we speak out of our own biases and limited knowledge."[19]

19. Sarah Travis, *Decolonizing Preaching: The Pulpit as Postcolonial Space* (Eugene, OR: Wipf & Stock, 2014), 97.

Second, we encourage preachers to gather people for a Bible study focused on the Sunday's preaching passage. Instead of telling participants what the story means, preachers can invite them into discussion and creative practices that motivate them to engage the story and offer possible connections to their own lives.[20] This Bible study will give preachers a sense of what hearers already know about the story and what they desire to know. It helps to identify the particular story within the grand biblical narrative that needs to be addressed; that is, a sermon's specific focus.

Sermonic Loglines

We urge preachers to develop a logline for each sermon in order to assist with the focus of the sermon. For example, a preacher might land on the following logline for a sermon based on Psalm 23: "The Holy Spirit meets people exactly where they are in their lives, even, perhaps especially, those who are in deep despair." This statement is essentially a sermonic logline, which helps the preacher swiftly describe the sermon to others. If the logline is unclear or cumbersome, preachers will need to refine it.

For the filmmaker, the logline is primarily used to market a film. For the preacher, it can be a guide in the sermon-crafting process. Marvin McMickle notes that this sermonic claim "helps sort through all of the things that could be said in any one sermon, and helps to narrow the preacher's focus down to what should and will be said in this particular sermon."[21] Ultimately, everything in the sermon, as with a film, should then be connected to the logline and contribute to the desired impact on the audience. McMickle refers to Fred Craddock, who said,

20. For more ways to tune into the lives of hearers relative to preaching practices and to invite them into the process, see Shauna Hannan, *The Peoples' Sermon: Preaching as a Ministry of the Whole Congregation*, Working Preacher Books (Minneapolis: Fortress Press, 2021).

21. Marvin A. McMickle, *Shaping the Claim: Moving from Text to Sermon*, Elements of Preaching (Minneapolis: Fortress Press, 2008), Kindle loc. 113–14. This statement is akin to what homileticians regularly encourage preachers to write when moving "from text to sermon." Thomas Long's "focus statement" is "a concise description of the central, controlling, and unifying theme of the sermon." See Long, *The Witness of Preaching*, 3rd ed. (Louisville, KY: Westminster John Knox Press, 2016), 127.

To aim at nothing is to miss everything, but to be specific and clear in one's presentation is to make direct contact with many whose ages, circumstances, and apparent needs are widely divergent. Listeners to sharply focused sermons have an amazing capacity to perceive that the sermon was prepared with them specifically in mind.[22]

While there is already a sermonic equivalent to a cinematic logline, the focus statement, filmmaking does not have an industry-wide term for an impact statement. Preaching does. The "function statement," as Thomas Long calls it, is "a description of what the preacher hopes the sermon will create or cause to happen for the hearers. . . . The function statement names the hoped-for change."[23] For each sermon, Long encourages preachers to write a one-sentence function statement that describes what a preacher wants the sermon to do to or for the hearers in light of what the biblical text does and in light of what is known about the hearers and their lives. In other words, the preacher identifies the hoped-for impact of the sermon on individual hearers, the church, and maybe even the world. Perhaps one might call this a "functional logline."

Given the sample logline above (The Holy Spirit meets people exactly where they are in their lives, even, perhaps especially, those who are in deep despair), possible functional loglines for a sermon based on Psalm 23 might be:

— This sermon aims to comfort hearers by letting them know that the Holy Spirit is accompanying them in their grief.
— This sermon will assure hearers that while the way to newfound hope is through mourning, their weeping will one day turn to dancing.

A functional logline is not an end in itself but a means to an end— an end that aims to impact the life of the viewer, listener, or reader. Note how the writer of the Gospel of Luke begins by indicating the hoped-for impact on the message's recipients:

Since many have undertaken to compile a narrative about the events that have been fulfilled among us, just as they were handed

22. McMickle, *Shaping the Claim*, Kindle loc. 115–17, quotes Fred B. Craddock, *Preaching* (Nashville: Abingdon, 1985), 155.
23. Long, *Witness of Preaching*, 127.

on to us by those who from the beginning were eyewitnesses and servants of the word, I, too, decided, as one having a grasp of everything from the start, to write a well-ordered account for you, most excellent Theophilus, so that you may have a firm grasp of the words in which you have been instructed. (Luke 1:1–4 NRSVue)

Why, preachers, do you wish to tell God's story? What is the hoped-for impact of your proclamation? Perhaps it is so that others "may have a firm grasp of the words in which you have been instructed." Or, perhaps, it is so that your hearers may feel beloved and valued by their creator. Other possibilities might be to empower people to serve their neighbor or to challenge systemic injustices—in other words, to live differently. For each sermon, will you want primarily for your hearers to *know* something? to *feel* something? to *do* something?

Individual sermons are often based on one portion of this story even as they aim to align with the broader story. When amassed over time, the cumulative effect of a body of sermons is more than the sum of its parts. That is to say, no individual sermon can do it all. Not even the cumulative effect can exhaust the depth and breadth of the story. And yet we try. Why? Because it makes a difference; it has an impact. Preachers hope to impact people's lives. Sermons can do things.[24]

Even though there may not be an equivalent film industry term for function statement, the desired impact on the audience permeates every choice the filmmaking team makes from writing to shooting to editing, including selecting the genre of the film. So too for the preacher, the functional logline can affect the kind of content in the sermon.

The Sermon and Film Genre

Determined by a film's style, theme, plot, conventions, and character types, the primary film genres are action-adventure, comedy, documentary, drama, fantasy, film noir, horror, romance, sci-fi, and thriller. One might ask which genre is most suitable for preachers to pay attention to. We think preachers can find connections between the Bible and each of the film genres. You may utilize wisdom from one or more genres in a sermon, depending on its desired impact.

---

24. Intentionality can be Spirit-led and therefore need not be equated with manipulation, as some may be led to believe.

The documentary, with its desire to chronicle past, present, and future experiences, seems to be an obvious possibility. It's the "factual" nature of God's presence in our lives that the preacher hopes will impact listeners. Often unscripted, nonfiction films such as documentaries can throw shade or light on a subject; expose different lives, living situations, and points of view (POVs); or illuminate a historical period or event in order to educate, instruct, or simply bear witness to events by documenting them. Ken Burns's miniseries *The U.S. and the Holocaust* (2022) recounted how antisemitism was baked into US culture and government during Hitler's rise and World War II. Consider also the home movie, which is a type of personal documentary that puts hearers front and center as they see and hear themselves.

Sermons can also be like *dramas,* with their ability to show every type of human emotion, struggle, conflict, and relationship; to conjure villains, heroes, and antiheroes; and to take us to other worlds and times, from the past to the future. We find an example with the first two seasons of *The White Lotus* (2021–) as it pulls audiences into the world of affluence and service industry workers.

Learning from character-driven films could benefit preachers because, essentially, every sermon is a character study of God. When an audience absorbs the spectrum of human actions and reactions of a lead character, often breathing in sync with them, it is moved and motivated on many levels. The feature drama *Tár* (2022), which depicted the rise and fall of a symphony conductor, challenged audiences to ponder themes of gender, cancel culture, art, and power.

Romance may not be the first genre people think of when looking for help with preaching. Yet it could be said that the biblical story functions like a love story between God and God's beloved creation.

And what should we say about *horror*? No doubt the Bible is filled with stories of betrayal, destruction, violence, and murder. In chapter 2 of his expansive book on genre, *The Anatomy of Genres,* John Truby begins his study with horror because "the major distinction governing human existence is life versus death." He says that "Genesis in the Old Testament is where horror elements first come together as a genre."[25] But should preachers look to the horror genre for tips on impactful preaching? In her now classic feminist manifesto, theologian Phyllis Trible acknowledges that "scripture reflects [life] in both holiness and horror." She goes on to say that "reflections themselves neither man-

25. John Truby, *The Anatomy of Genres: How Story Forms Explain the Way the World Works* (New York: Picador, 2022), 22.

date nor manufacture change; yet by enabling insight, they may inspire repentance. In other words, sad stories may yield new beginnings."[26] In the introductory chapter, "On Telling Sad Stories," Trible says that her task in writing the book is

> to tell sad stories as I hear them. Indeed, they are tales of terror with women as victims. Belonging to the sacred scriptures of synagogue and church, these narratives yield four portraits of suffering in ancient Israel: Hagar, the slave used, abused, and rejected; Tamar, the princess raped and discarded; an unnamed woman, the concubine raped, murdered, and dismembered; and the daughter of Jephthah, a virgin slain and sacrificed.[27]

Trible's approach "recounts tales of terror *in memoriam* to offer sympathetic readings to abused women" and "interprets stories of outrage on behalf of their female victims in order to recover a neglected history, to remember a past that the present embodies, and to pray that these terrors shall not come to pass again."[28] With a nod to Paul Ricœur, she says, "If without stories we live not, stories live not without us. Alone a text is mute and ineffectual. In the speaking and the hearing new things appear on the land."[29] While we might leave the "land of terror," we do so, Trible says, with a limp.

But a question remains: what attracts people to horror films? Author John Lyden engages the work of theologian Jon Pahl, who argues that "what viewers enjoy is surviving the ordeals witnessed onscreen: 'A viewer is, experientially, resurrected by enduring a terrifying identification with the death of a victim and then walking out of the theatre alive' as horror films 'condense the fear of death into a cinematic spectacle that displaces fear onto various actors in traumatic circumstances' after which the viewer is 'saved' by a return to the 'real world.'" Lyden concludes that "the liminal experience is itself cathartic in the mere fact that one can leave the theater whole—and even laugh off the fear."[30]

26. Phyllis Trible, *Texts of Terror: Literary-Feminist Readings of Biblical Narratives* (Philadelphia: Fortress Press, 1984), 2.

27. Trible, *Texts of Terror*, 1.

28. Trible, *Texts of Terror*, 3.

29. Trible, *Texts of Terror*, 1.

30. John C. Lyden, *Film as Religion: Myths, Morals, and Rituals*, 2nd ed. (New York: New York University Press, 2019), 218. Lyden is quoting Jon Pahl, *Empire of Sacrifice: The Religious Origins of American Violence* (New York: New York University Press, 2010), 55.

Perhaps herein lies the usefulness of film's horror genre for the preacher. We are left to ask if, like the horror film genre, sermons might provide space for people to express and master their fears.[31] If Scott Derrickson is correct when he calls horror "the genre of non-denial," it is worth a closer look if preachers adhere to a theology of the cross that aims to "call a thing what it really is."[32]

One challenge to a preacher's engagement with certain film genres is the notion of truth telling. People might give more leeway to film-makers to "make up" stories. However, the expectation of preachers is that what they say is true. Indeed, there is a long history of deductive preaching that aims to persuade hearers of the truth of a claim. Even so, with the rise of the New Homiletic in the late 1960s and the emergence of inductive preaching, the goal has become less about persuasion and more about transformation. Preachers can learn from the ways film-makers tell stories that are factual, entirely fiction, or "based on true events."

The Sermon and Film Format

Beyond the discussion of genre is the question of format, source, and medium. Given that preachers are beginning with an original source, an existing text, the Bible, and adapting its message for a different medium, the sermon, it seems useful to reflect on *adapted screenplays* as a model. An adapted screenplay is a film sourced from and based on an original work first offered in another medium (e.g., novel or play). The challenge for filmmakers adapting an original text is to preserve the tone and themes from the original work as they change elements to better suit the medium. Sound familiar, preachers? One might then study films based on the biblical story, as noted above.

Preachers, however, could learn just as much by broadening the focus to other adapted screenplays, such as *West Side Story,* with its multiple and varied adaptations. Inspired by William Shakespeare's *Romeo and Juliet,* Arthur Laurent made it into a "book musical" before Jerome Robbins and Leonard Bernstein adapted it into a theatrical

---

31. See Brigid Cherry, "Refusing to Refuse to Look," in *Identifying Hollywood's Audiences: Cultural Identity and the Movies,* ed. Melvyn Stokes and Richard Maltby (London: British Film Institute, 1999), 187–203.

32. In Josh Larsen, *Fear Not! A Christian Appreciation of Horror Movies* (Eugene, OR: Cascade Books, 2023), 6. On the theology of the cross, see Martin Luther's Heidelberg Disputation.

performance in the 1950s. Since then, *West Side Story* has been represented on the stage numerous times and in numerous countries. Imagine all the challenges and possibilities of recontextualizing it for each iteration. *West Side Story* was first adapted into a film in 1961 and then readapted in 2021. This point should also resonate for preachers. Comparing the various iterations is like comparing multiple sermons on the same biblical passage preached sixty years apart. Imagination and contextualization abound in the interpretations even as the creators attempt to remain faithful to the original and have an impact on the present-day context. We preachers know how our primary story ends (at least, the written part). The challenge is how we weave it into the twenty-first century. Same story—new era, new audience.

So far we've been highlighting the feature-length film, but there are other program formats, both short and extended, worth exploring. Whether it's an adaptation or an original, consider which format (meaning the structure of the story in terms of its program length, a.k.a. running time) fits all that is intended. Will the sermon be completed in a single telling akin to a long-form feature film or a short-form film or video? Or does it call for being spun out over multiple tellings, like TV episodes or a miniseries? The short film, for example, is more aligned with sermon length and, therefore, can be instructive in the way it moves through the plot quickly.[33] Keeping with this idea of length and rapid movement within each show and its episodic rhythm, one could say the television series is more similar to preaching. Each episode serves the impact of the overall series by moving along the plot, complexifying the problems, giving clues to the solutions, and, above all, withholding and revealing features of characters. In *The Homiletic of All Believers,* O. Wesley Allen Jr., writes, "As with script writing, preachers must have a bifocal approach to developing sermons—to preach effective individual sermons that *cumulatively* influence the community's proclamatory conversations and individuals' meaning-making processes."[34] Might our week-to-week sermons be binge-worthy?

33. See works by Eugene Lowry, such as *The Homiletical Plot: The Sermon as Narrative Art Form; The Homiletical Beat: Why All Sermons Are Narrative;* and *Doing Time in the Pulpit: The Relationship between Narrative and Preaching.*

34. O. Wesley Allen, Jr., *The Homiletic of All Believers: A Conversational Approach to Proclamation and Preaching* (Louisville, KY: Westminster John Knox Press, 2005), 61; emphasis added. Allen uses the analogy of television series to illustrate the impact sought in cumulative preaching (58–64).

Sermon Form and Impact

The gamut of genres available to the filmmaker is somewhat akin to the variety of sermon forms available to the preacher. Preachers often land on a sermon form by subject matter and occasion, but the sermon form could also be chosen relative to desired impact. Just like the unfortunate tendency to generalize about a film genre (for example, rom-coms entertain and docs inform), one might generalize about the impact of a particular sermon form. For instance, a deductive sermon (a traditional three-point form) informs and therefore might be chosen when aiming to teach something about a particular church doctrine. Or an inductive sermon (much like Eugene Lowry's narrative "homiletical plot," a.k.a. Lowry's Loop) might be chosen when aiming to invite the audience into an experience (e.g., of being forgiven or liberated). However, like film genre, each sermon form does so much more.

Another important consideration is which form best suits the occasion of the sermon. Funerals are typically (though not necessarily) serious and sad whereas festivals (like Christmas and Easter) are celebratory. On more ordinary Sundays, the tone and character of the biblical passage likely drive the form. Biblical stories produce a gamut of experiences; they can delight, inform, redirect, amuse, comfort, challenge, convict. The list goes on. Preachers begin by noticing the impact a biblical story has on themselves and others (in the presermon Bible study, for instance) and aim for the sermon to have a similar impact. In each of these scenarios, the audience and their needs are front and center in the sermon-crafting process.[35]

Above all, the "how" of preaching is just as important as the "what." Sermon form itself adds a layer of meaning. Beyond simply being a way of structuring the parts of the sermon, it is an invitation for how to hear, how to receive the message, and, in that way, is an act of pastoral care.[36] We address this more in chapter 5 on editing.

How to Gauge Actual Impact

Gauging a sermon's impact is neither quick nor easy. The congregation's offering plate is not the filmmaker's box office. While the cumulative

---

35. For more information on various sermon forms and their impact, see O. Wesley Allen, Jr., *Determining the Form* (Minneapolis: Fortress Press, 2018).

36. Long, *Witness of Preaching*, 150.

effect of weekly sermons is the best way to measure homiletical impact (one documentarian called the cinematic equivalent "the longitudinal impact"[37]), preachers have a lot to gain from gauging the impact of individual sermons. Taking a cue from filmmakers, for starters, don't wait until after you've preached the sermon.

"Prerelease" Screening

Preachers would do well to consider doing their own kind of test marketing before they preach a sermon. "As preachers put words to paper, they can test certain sections with some listeners, carefully observing whether and how impact matches intent."[38] Another book in this "Preaching and . . ." book series, *Preaching and the Thirty-Second Commercial*, affirms this process:

> Advertisers' use of market segmentation and focus groups expands preachers' tools for understanding their congregation and emphatically constructing what they need from a sermon. Tools such as these help the preacher avoid general messages delivered to a general audience and instead target their particular congregation with a particularly significant message drawn from a particular biblical text.[39]

This process can be imaginary. However, conversations in real time with actual people are preferred, for reasons noted above. HyeRan Kim-Cragg also cautions against preachers making assumptions: "The close examination of and attention to preachers' own places become critical when diverse experience in the pew and that in the pulpit are in conflict."[40] She affirms that "preaching is never a solitary act. It involves people; people from the congregation, people outside the church, and even creation itself."[41] Sarah Travis speaks of "the always partial truth of

37. Michele Stephenson, "Doctalk Panel," Docland Film Festival, San Rafael, CA, October 14, 2023.

38. Hannan, *Peoples' Sermon*, 94.

39. O. Wesley Allen, Jr., and Carrie La Ferle, *Preaching and the Thirty-Second Commercial: Lessons from Advertising for the Pulpit* (Louisville, KY: Westminster John Knox Press, 2021), 47. Allen and La Ferle address the importance of moving beyond making broad assumptions through market research focus groups; see p. 42.

40. HyeRan Kim-Cragg, *Postcolonial Preaching: Creating a Ripple Effect* (Lanham, MD: Lexington Books, 2021), 55.

41. Kim-Cragg, *Postcolonial Preaching*, 58.

the preacher" since "there are limits to our ability to fully know others, let alone speak for others."[42] Travis seeks to decolonize preaching by not assuming we can "imagine" others.

So imagining is a start, but it does not go far enough. The filmic equivalent is something like the Bechdel Test, which measures actual female roles and participation. How much more important this is for the preacher who wishes to be representative of the variety of hearers in order for the gospel to ring true for them.

Sermon Impact Teams

While many preachers learn to embrace the need to identify their sermon's hoped-for impact, far fewer preachers embrace the encouragement to find out what impact a sermon actually has on their hearers. We encourage congregations to create impact teams (maybe even have an impact producer?) in order to maximize a sermon's impact, even its potential for social change.[43] Impact teams can

— help preachers "read" the audience;
— have their "ears to the ground" in ways that preachers cannot;
— serve as test hearers for certain sections of sermons, which can be particularly beneficial when a preacher sees fit to challenge hearers with prophetic proclamation; and
— begin to hear sermons differently because they are engaged at a different level; they may even develop confidence and competence to "spread the word" in a whole new way.

It doesn't take a blockbuster budget for preachers to adopt feedback practices to find out how hearers receive their sermons. Preachers, in cooperation with impact team members, can establish rhythms for finding out quickly what impact their preaching has on hearers. Consider these possibilities:

— Solicit responses to two or three written feedback questions on the back of the bulletin or on social media.

42. Travis, *Decolonizing Preaching*, 103.
43. See Shauna Hannan, "Impact Teams," in "What Preachers Can Learn from Filmmakers," Wabash Center for Teaching and Learning (2019–20), https://www.wabashcenter.wabash.edu/2020/02/what-preachers-can-learn-from-filmmakers-part-2-of-4-impact-teams/.

—Designate one table at the coffee hour following worship as the sermon roundtable where members of the sermon impact team facilitate conversation.

It is important to remember that this occasion is not for the preacher to receive ego strokes or ego strikes. Instead, consider asking simply, "What happened to you during the sermon today?" or "What in particular made this experience happen for you?" With a bit of coaching, congregation members will soon embrace the power of the pulpit for their lives.[44]

What William Romanowski says about the benefits of "spirited post-movie discussions" can apply to postsermon discussions. "We become better critics with deeper self-awareness through spirited post-movie discussions that make us consider our values, refine our point of view, and sometimes challenge us to think differently."[45] These postsermon discussions may even change our behavior for good.

SUMMARY

Filmmakers want to create something that makes an audience react. Film critic Roger Ebert said that film is an "empathy machine." Indeed, filmmakers want something to happen to the viewer. "Apathy is our worst enemy," says filmmaker Jason Wilkinson. "'Good' or 'Bad' equals success. Indifference equals failure."[46] The same may be true of the preacher's creation, the sermon. Preachers want something to happen to the hearers. While rarely does a single sermon move mountains, it can move us.

The next chapter explores the necessity of collaboration in both filmmaking and preaching in order to achieve the desired impact.

---

44. Hannan, *Peoples' Sermon*, 131–57.
45. Romanowski, *Cinematic Faith*, 26.
46. Author (Hannan) conversation with Wilkinson.

2

Cast and Crew: Collaborating for Impact

COLLABORATIVE FILMMAKING

Collaboration is indispensable for filmmakers; they are not solo artists. Ron Howard says that the best part of being a film director is that "the director . . . [really gets] to play with everybody."[1] Filmmakers know that it takes many people to create an experience, to have an impact. Directors simply cannot do it all on their own. Therefore they hire talent (the cast) and crew, including the location scout, cinematographer, set designer, costume designer, editor, and a host of others. Even on low-budget films where directors do more by necessity, they depend on their cast and crew to work for free or on an *if / come* basis (with pay contingent on the film being sold).

Still there is a lasting theory of filmmaking that ignores the collaborative aspects and posits that every film has a solo visionary. In the early 1950s, avant-garde French filmmakers fed up with Hollywood techniques and subjects became hell-bent on designing a new national cinema focused on the lives of everyday French people, not just the bourgeoisie. They fomented La Nouvelle Vague (The New Wave) of filmmaking and formulated the *auteur theory*, which holds that the true

---

1. Marcia McFee, *Think like a Filmmaker: Sensory-Rich Worship Design for Unforgettable Messages* (Truckee, CA: Tokay Press, 2016), 43. McFee references a video interview with Howard available on YouTube, "Ron Howard's Advice," February 21, 2013, https://www.youtube.com/watch?v=XOxItKRzPOY.

author (auteur) of a film is not the screenwriter but a director with a distinct style. Prime examples include Alfred Hitchcock, John Ford, Howard Hawks, and Orson Welles, whom the New Wave filmmakers revered.

Director Martin Brest critiques auteur theory when he asserts that "the personality of a particular film cannot be solely attributed to one person." He argues,

> It was interesting there for a while having the director be considered God, but now that it's out that he [sic] isn't, we've all survived. . . . To me, I look at the job as trying to get the most out of all the people you work with, trying to get them to do things beyond what they might normally do. And the better you are at doing that, then the better all people you're working with, actors, technicians and craftsmen [sic], will be at their jobs. And by definition, that seems to contradict any theory of the director as sole author of a film.[2]

Roles and Responsibilities

Filmmaking, including film directing, is all about collaboration—interdependence and placing trust in others. Everyone has a job to do in bringing the story to life. At its best, it's a stimulating intersection of minds and creativities as writers, actors, and the entire crew down to craft service (the person who sets up the snack table and aids other crafts on set) partner to deliver the film. Whether the end product is a movie, television show, or music video, everyone contributes and is part of a well-oiled operation.[3] Relationships strengthen as new projects bring together the same team for continued collaborations.

The table below shows the roles and responsibilities of a film's cast (those seen in front of the camera) and crew (those unseen behind the camera). It includes some of the problems these filmmakers would face by identifying questions they would address. The list is arranged in workflow order. Two or more roles can be filled by one person,

2. Michael Singer, *A Cut Above: 50 Film Directors Talk about Their Craft* (Los Angeles: Lone Eagle Publishing, 1998), 21.

3. Of course, there are films that people create on their own with no or minimal help, e.g., YouTube videos, TikTok videos, home movies, and low-budget shows, such as wedding videos, training videos, and in-house corporate projects.

such as writer-directors, actor-producer-directors, director-editors, and so on. While roles may overlap, responsibilities don't change: the producer is the high-ranking manager who keeps the show on track; the director is the creative that turns the script into engaging images, sounds, characters, and so on. As film credits affirm, there are many more crew jobs, but those listed here constitute the major roles and those most relevant to preachers. Consider how you would fill in the preaching equivalent in terms of roles, responsibilities, and problems to be solved.

Role	Questions Filmmakers Address	Responsibilities and Impact
Screenwriter	What story do I want to tell? What character(s) do I want to write about? What themes, plots, settings, and time periods intrigue or concern me?	To create the final shooting script from inception through collaboration with director and producer on multiple drafts. Impacts the story and how it's told, including its genre and format as well as its setting(s) and character(s).
Producer	Can we shoot the crowd scene in a day? Is the director delivering? Can we afford a composer?	To shepherd the entire show by hiring key personnel, such as the director, overseeing the budget, and keeping everything on track from script to the final show deliverables. Impacts the show by making sure it's completed and delivered on time.
Director	Is any of this working? This actor is miscast; what can I do? Will everything cut together?	To hold the vision for how to tell the story with images, sound, and emotional engagement from the first roll of the camera to the last edit of the final cut. Impacts every aspect of the show that the audience sees.
Talent (Actor)	Is this true to my character? Did I hit my mark? What would my character do here? How can I best communicate with my words, face, eyes, and body?	To interpret their character (fiction shows) or tell their experience (nonfiction shows) with the guidance of the director who understands the scope and vision of the entire project. Impacts show by inhabiting the character and eliciting audience reactions.

continued on next page

Role	Questions Filmmakers Address (cont.)	Responsibilities and Impact (cont.)
Director of Photography	How shall we light this scene? What focal length should the camera be? Should we use a drone for the opening shot?	To visually translate the director's intentions for story, character, setting, and mood for each scene via camera moves, settings, and framing along with lighting and color palette choices. Impacts the look and lighting of the film by being its composer.
Set Designer	Does this really feel like 1892? 2192? Does this room fit the character? How will lighting affect the materials I'm contemplating using?	To research, invent, and create the environment for each scene and setting by conferring with the director and producer and communicating with wardrobe, lighting, prop, and other departments. Impacts the look and feel of each location and set to make the environment, and thereby the story, believable.
Sound Recordist	Is the take's sound clean: no dog barking in the background, clothes rustling, dolly squeak, or other unwanted noise? Do characters talk over one another or is their dialogue clear?	To record clean tracks that will edit well and that the audience can clearly understand. To record ambience (ambient sound) on set and for each location. To anticipate audio that will be needed in editing to tell the story and realize the director's soundscape vision. Impacts the show by capturing the sounds that sound editors will use to design and craft the show's aural world.
Editor	This scene drags: What can I do? This doc makes no sense: How can we pull the narrative together? The helicopter overhead drowns out the words: Can I marry the picture from one take with the dialogue from another?	To put together the footage to best tell the story through cuts of different lengths. To work with the sound, not just so that dialogue can be heard or music can augment emotion but to put viewers in an aural landscape, be it the present, past, or future, so that they accept the film's reality. Impacts the show by being its final writer and helping to guide the editing process.

Phases of Filmmaking: Adding Collaborators as You Go

Filmmaking can be a solo endeavor in which one person scripts, shoots, and edits the entire show, but this is not the norm, and it occurs primarily on short films. The majority of films are created through collaborative effort. It takes hundreds of people to produce a major motion picture, a minimal crew of a dozen or so to make a low-budget show. The traditional Hollywood workflow starts with a scriptwriter writing the screenplay and soliciting feedback from other filmmakers along the way. Once the script is *green-lit* (given the go-ahead by a studio), additional writer(s) may be assigned, and the movie enters development. On television series, where multiple writers are the norm, the writing team will gather at the start of the season and/or beginning of an episode to blue sky (brainstorm) ideas for plots, scenes, and characters. Anything goes during these brainstorming, freewriting sessions. At least one writer got into the business after watching Rob, Sally, and Buddy kibbitz in the writer's room on *The Dick Van Dyke Show*. While the script continues to be polished, producers, director, casting director, principle talent (actors, interviewees, and/or experts), storyboard artist, and others come on board.

The number of collaborators burgeons during preproduction as department heads are hired—for example, set designer, DP (director of photography, or cinematographer), wardrobe, makeup, props—and location scouts are deployed. An artist creates a *storyboard*. The storyboard, with its shot-by-shot drawings of the action in each scene, is an immense aid to the director, set designer, and DP, who study it to visualize shots, scenes, and characters' actions. The storyboard can be used to rearrange scenes and save time and money during production. Based on her work with the producer-director-editor brothers Ethan and Joel Coen, actor Frances McDormand believes in the pre- and postproduction visualizing powers of storyboarding: "I always ask directors if they do storyboards. . . . I find it a valuable thing even if I never see them. . . . I believe it's an editor's medium so as an actor if I'm serving the final edit of the film which I believe storyboards prepare you for, then I know the person [director] knows what they're doing."[4]

During production, or the shoot, crews are filled out as script supervisor, sound recordist, gaffer (head of lighting), stunt coordinator, editorial, and more are added. Following the shoot, in postproduction (*editing* or post), the production crew's job is done, but the work of the

---

4. "Storyboarding *Blood Simple*," Criterion Collection, September 19, 2016, https://www.youtube.com/watch?v=MsGRhaPpGh0.

picture and sound editors and the *VFX* (video effects) crew is ramping up. You get the picture: Filmmaking depends on a number—often a great number, as head and tail credits reflect—of people working together, collaborating to get the show *in the can* (completely filmed) and delivered.

Still, with all these dedicated cast and crew, the creative vision primarily rests with one person. On feature films, the director holds the vision; on TV shows it's the creator, also called *showrunner*, or executive producer, like David E. Kelley (*Ally McBeal, The Practice, Big Sky*) and Shonda Rhimes (*Grey's Anatomy, Scandal, Bridgerton*). There certainly is a hierarchy in filmmaking, but a solo endeavor? Not usually. Everyone is taking input, desired or not: film crew heads (cinematographer, music composer, editor, etc.) from the director, director from producer(s), producer(s) from studio exec(s); all from the audience members who vote with their theater ticket, TV remote, or computer mouse.

Mundane and Magical

> Art is technology. It's the one thing that you can do . . . to communicate emotion from one human being to another human being. . . . Whether you're telling stories, you're telling plays, you're doing music, you're writing books, you're painting pictures, it's all about the technology.
> —George Lucas[5]

Every role in filmmaking is both mundane and magical, technical and artistic. For instance, an actor has to show up at least an hour before being required on set to be prepared by hair, makeup, and wardrobe departments; a DP will spend time trying out equipment and running lighting tests; and an editor will need hours to input the footage into a *digital editing system* and organize it before even beginning to edit. These are the mundane tasks that must be done. On the magic side, an editor will drop in a piece of music and suddenly a scene will zing with added meaning; a cinematographer will capture the light and the subject in a way that imprints it in the audience's consciousness; and an actor will inhabit a character that stays with viewers long after the credits fade and the house lights appear.

5. George Lucas, interview by Senator Bill Bradley, *American Voices*, March 7, 2012, Sirius XM Stars.

COLLABORATIVE PREACHING

Much like the French filmmakers of the mid-twentieth century who downplayed collaborative aspects of filmmaking, there is a theory that preachers are the sole visionaries of their sermons. Unfortunately, this theory has made its way into practice. Some likely think a sermon comes to be simply by standing up in the pulpit and receiving direct inspiration from the Spirit. More likely, people imagine a preacher spending hour upon hour in an office studying Scripture and crafting a polished fifteen- to forty-five-minute speech. Either way, it has come to be understood and practiced as a solo endeavor in which the preacher is like a low-budget filmmaker who is the screenwriter, director, producer, editor, and marketer as well as the popcorn maker. Indeed, this process has worked. And likely it will continue to work in some communities, albeit at the expense of missed opportunities for maximum impact.

Possibilities abound when more people are involved in the creative process of sermon crafting. Marcia McFee highlights the filmmaker's way of embracing collaboration for worship planning. "If liturgy literally means 'work of the people,' then let's put the people to work."[6] Her book *Think like a Filmmaker* encourages worship planners to go about the same type of intentional teamwork as filmmakers do. Prompted by Ron Howard's quote at the beginning of this chapter, McFee writes, "Teamwork is the name of the game in filmmaking, and it can make or break the experience of creating a film. No one person can do it alone—it takes a group of people with a shared vision cast by a director they trust to lead the creative process through a production timeline."[7] Where worship planning teams are de rigueur for some communities, the sermon is still considered a solo act.

Even the preacher as low-budget filmmaker is collaborative. Quite often preachers connect with other preachers to study the lectionary Scripture readings. Or (and often also) they engage with a wider variety of scholarly voices in the form of written commentaries. And, of course, just as a speaker needs a hearer in any communication event, a preacher needs a congregation of listeners. So, yes, in these ways there is collaboration. But imagine the possibilities if preachers acted like film directors who pull together a team and get to "play with everybody" on that team. The sermon needs a director, yes, but also a cast and

6. McFee, *Think like a Filmmaker*, 43.
7. McFee, *Think like a Filmmaker*, 43.

crew. Broader teamwork offers the best chance of achieving the greatest impact.

Various Collaborative Homiletics

A collaborative approach to preaching is not a new concept. Numerous homiletics professors in recent decades have proposed a collaborative approach to sermon preparation.[8] Lucy Atkinson Rose identifies examples that go back to the mid-twentieth century:

> To facilitate dialogue between the preacher and the congregation, [Clyde] Reid suggests pre-sermon Bible study groups and post-sermon discussion groups. Gene E. Bartlett claims that the active participation of the congregation while a sermon is being preached has not been taken seriously enough. . . . He calls on preachers to envision the worshiper in the pew as "a subject acting, not an object acted upon."[9]

Dietrich Ritschl's warning in the 1960s was clear: "Part of the cruelty (which we ourselves have created) of our Church is that minister and congregation are separated in such a way that the preacher is alone and isolated with [the] preaching task."[10] With a less alarming tone, in the 1980s theologian Martin Marty asked preachers, "Have you thought what a great part the people *may* play in weak or faulty preaching? What about the part people *must* play in preaching which works its fuller effect?" He admits, "I have been moved to learn something: the message has greatest effect when it is most clear that the people with whom I am a hearer are participating in preaching. They are 'preaching *with* . . .'"[11]

---

8. Parts of this section first appeared in Shauna Hannan, *The Peoples' Sermon* (Minneapolis: Fortress Press, 2021). See especially the introduction and chap. 3, "The Case for Collaboration."

9. Lucy Atkinson Rose, *Sharing the Word: Preaching in the Roundtable Church* (Louisville, KY: Westminster John Knox Press, 1997), 39.

10. Dietrich Ritschl, *A Theology of Proclamation* (Richmond: John Knox Press, 1960), 15–16.

11. Martin Marty, *The Word: People Participating in Preaching* (Philadelphia: Fortress Press, 1984), 15, 19.

In the 1990s, Episcopal priest Barbara Brown Taylor proposed that "preaching is not something an ordained minister does for fifteen minutes on Sundays but what the whole congregation does all week long; it is a way of approaching the world and of gleaning God's presence there."[12] During that same era, other members of the Academy of Homiletics pushed toward collaborative preaching (in its many possible forms). Especially notable was the work of two preaching professors from the Presbyterian Church (U.S.A.) who wrote homiletical textbooks that emphasized preaching as a collaborative venture. John McClure advocated for collaborative sermon roundtables in order to help the preacher take sermon preparation "out of the pastoral study and into the context of roundtable conversation."[13] Lucy Atkinson Rose proposed a conversational preaching model that is "communal, nonhierarchical, personal, inclusive, and scriptural." She encourages "a nonhierarchical, communal relationship between pastor and congregation that questions traditional assumptions of preaching, and offers insight from those on the margin and those outside the field of homiletics."[14]

Nearly a decade later (2005), United Methodist scholar O. Wesley Allen, Jr., picked up Rose's proposal and wrote *The Homiletic of All Believers: A Conversational Approach to Proclamation and Preaching,* in which he outlines a "conversational ecclesiology and homiletic."[15]

Yet another decade passed before David Lose of the Evangelical Lutheran Church in America wondered, "If our people have spent their entire lives watching others [preachers] talk about faith but have never themselves had an opportunity to do so, where will they have developed the competence and confidence to do it themselves?"[16] Lose builds on what a fellow Lutheran, Herman Stuempfle, noted decades earlier: preaching's purpose is to equip lay people for their missionary

12. Barbara Brown Taylor, *The Preaching Life* (Lanham, MD: Rowman & Littlefield, 1993), 32.

13. John McClure, *The Roundtable Pulpit: Where Leadership and Preaching Meet* (Nashville: Abingdon, 1995).

14. Rose, *Sharing the Word,* 121 and back cover.

15. O. Wesley Allen, Jr., *The Homiletic of All Believers: A Conversational Approach to Proclamation and Preaching* (Louisville, KY: Westminster John Knox Press, 2005).

16. David Lose, *Preaching at the Crossroads: How the World—and Our Preaching—Is Changing* (Minneapolis: Fortress Press, 2013), 104–5.

work in the world.[17] Stuempfle recognized the effective power at work in the important role of "lay amplifiers scattered in every corner of society." Because "the preacher's voice *by itself* has limited carrying power," it is the listeners of the sermon who, in turn, "incarnate [God's] grace and truth in the whole range of their common life." Stuempfle asserts, "The first business of the individual preacher is to enable the Church to preach."[18] Enabling the church to preach is precisely the impetus for the book *The Peoples' Sermon,* which also argues in its third chapter that the emphasis on collaboration in industries and disciplines ranging from education to science to art to biology calls on preachers to embrace collaboration.

Roles and Responsibilities

Perhaps preachers can endorse this approach in theory but wonder what collaborative preaching looks like in practice. While some filmmaking roles and responsibilities do not correspond easily to a preacher's work (not many preachers have ordered a helicopter flyover for their sermon), many do have a homiletical equivalent. Here we propose collaborative roles that parallel filmmaking for both sermon preparation and delivery or embodiment.

Just as every role in filmmaking has elements that are mundane and magical as well as technical and artistic, the same is true in preaching. Take a moment to consider your sermon development and delivery process. Which elements are mundane? Which are magical? Which are technical? Artistic? Make a list of those around you who have such capabilities and then consider inviting them to be part of your homiletical cast and crew. Who are the creatives in your midst? Who has technical expertise? Whose artistic imagination does the congregation need to engage more? Identify the good listeners and the gracious critics. Call on the troubleshooters as well as the troublemakers. Then gather together your crew of what the apostle Paul might now call homiletical "co-laborers" (*synergoi*; 1 Cor. 3:9) What preacher does not want synergy between pulpit and pew?

17. Herman G. Stuempfle, *Preaching in the Witnessing Community* (Minneapolis: Fortress Press, 1973).
18. Stuempfle, *Preaching in the Witnessing Community*, vii. Emphasis added.

Preproduction Cast and Crew

Coscreenwriters

A commitment to "preaching *with*" begins in preproduction, that is, well before the sermon is preached. Tom Long reminds his readers that "sermon preparation is not just preparation for ministry, it is ministry."[19] If ministry is understood to be collaborative, and preaching is ministry, then sermon preparation should be the work of the community together rather than the work of one person.

A collaborative process (preaching *with* instead of *at*) begins with studying Scripture communally. United Methodist scholars Justo and Catherine González warn against "Lone Ranger preachers":

> The problem comes when we seem to say that [the preacher's] private Bible study is somehow better or deeper or more meaningful than corporate study—when we forget that the Bible comes out of a community and is addressed to a community. . . . Rather than encouraging their hearers to delve further into the Bible, [Lone Ranger preachers] are actually discouraging them. . . . The Bible becomes an esoteric book that only those with specialized education or gifts can possibly be able to understand. It is not a book for the lay Christian, but only for the "professional." This is hardly an attitude that should be encouraged in the church.[20]

Consider convening a group of people for a Bible study and opening up space for participants to offer ideas about the character development, the tone, the challenges, the discomfort, the grace that emerge in the story. From these explorations to other creative and collaborative exercises, you might discover in the participants coscreenwriters who can offer possible real-life illustrations of, for example, unexpected grace, long-awaited reconciliation, or life-giving hospitality. These coscreenwriters might then be open to including their stories in the sermon and, with their permission, becoming part of the congregation's homiletical cast, or talent pool. Building on Bible study, preachers can begin blue skying with certain congregation members. In filmmaking, to "blue sky" in "the writer's room" is to hold a brainstorming session

19. Thomas G. Long, *The Witness of Preaching*, 3rd ed. (Louisville, KY: Westminster John Knox Press, 2016), 265.

20. Justo and Catherine González, *The Liberating Pulpit* (Eugene, OR: Wipf & Stock, 1994), 47–50.

in which anyone is welcome to offer possibilities regarding the creative content of a film.

Coeditors

Who are the editors in your midst? That is, who might listen to sections of your sermon and give you feedback on what they hear, what excites them, what confuses them, what they want to know more about? Sometimes preachers get so close to their script that they cannot see the big picture. Trusted editors can assist with the broader trajectory as well as the fine print (individual sermon sections) or even finer print (phrasing and word choice). They can point out gaps, inconsistencies, and repetitions. They can aid with transitions from one section to another, as well as tease out sense and flow. They can also help with energy and tell you where things are bogging down. These "prerelease screenings" can provide a sense of whether the content of the sermon will connect and impact as intended and desired.

Casting Call: Broadening Talent Representation

Including others' input and perhaps even their stories in the sermon (always with explicitly stated permission!) can go a long way. But consider going one step further and inviting them to tell their own story at a designated point in the sermon. Being a part of the cast can broaden representation, literally enabling the church to preach.

Whose bodies are seen and heard during the sermon, and why does that matter? Consider these questions a kind of homiletical Bechdel Test. As more people speak and act during the sermon, the broader representation will honor diversity, encourage mutual influence, and create a sense of belonging. The filmmaking industry has made this a priority in recent years. The Motion Picture Association (MPA) states on its website that it is "committed to great storytelling that reflects the viewpoints and experiences of all creators and audiences—which is why we are working hard with our member studios to collectively address diversity, gender parity, *authentic* cultural representation, and pipeline recruitment opportunities from underrepresented communities in our industry."[21] The MPA hopes to lead by example. So can preachers.

21. "Advancing Diversity, Equity & Inclusion," What We Do, Motion Picture Association, accessed April 29, 2024, https://www.motionpictures.org /what-we-do/advancing-diversity-equity-inclusion/.

"Representation" is about the particularities of the people who are participating. Who is front and center in your worship settings? Who is seen and heard? Who seems to take the lead during preaching? Have you considered that a person's identity preaches? While not every congregation has the gift of a diverse pastoral staff, most congregations reflect some kind of diversity, whether in gender identity, age, race, sexual orientation, primary language, or other characteristics. Seeing the bodies and hearing the voices of this diverse representation connected to one of the church's quintessential practices, preaching, honors the diversity of God's beloved in more profound ways than simply saying, "The diversity of God's beloved is honored here." The complexity and diversity of human identity is the *imago Dei* at work.

We've recognized people's different "ways of knowing" and have therefore sought ways to avoid "the oppressive use of language that assumes there is only one way to see and respond to the vast and many-angled complexity of human life."[22] We've accepted that because "the preacher's experiences and articulations are never universal and normative, they need the corrective of the multiple experiences of God's people."[23] And yet, to "situate preaching as radical act of compassionate responsibility,"[24] we must move beyond seeking a corrective simply through awareness to actually expanding who is seen in and heard from the pulpit.[25] For when we honor people's particular identities and encourage their capacity to influence, they will likely experience a sense of belonging, which is a basic human need. Since one of the church's calls is arguably to care for basic human needs, we can add "offer a sense of belonging" to the essential list: feed the hungry, heal the sick, clothe the naked, visit the imprisoned. Where the structures of our practices implicitly (perhaps sometimes explicitly) contradict these aims, we have room to grow. Our preaching practices have room to grow.

22. Thomas H. Troeger and H. Edward Everding Jr., *So That All Might Know: Preaching That Engages the Whole Congregation* (Nashville: Abingdon Press, 2008), 7.

23. Rose, *Sharing the Word*, 125.

24. John McClure, *Other-Wise Preaching: A Postmodern Ethic for Homiletics* (St. Louis: Chalice, 2001), 7.

25. Elisabeth Schüssler Fiorenza proposes that "the clergy should relinquish their monopoly of the pulpit, since the right to preach derives from baptism and from each believer's experience of God." Rose (*Sharing the Word*, 97) refers to Elisabeth Schüssler Fiorenza, "Response," in *A New Look at Preaching*, ed. John Burke (Wilmington, DE: Michael Glazier, 1983), 48, 55.

From Homiletical Auteur to Varied Collaborators

The called preacher is still the key member of the cast as well as the crew, as a producer who oversees and manages the whole production and perhaps as the director whose creative vision drives the content.[26] Homiletical collaboration will not be shirking a preacher's responsibility for faithful preaching; it will in fact be fulfilling the responsibility to equip and empower the priesthood of all believers to proclaim. For we know that when a responsibility is shared it has a greater impact, since people move from being spectators to what Brazilian theater director Augusto Boal calls "spect-actors." And through this participation, audience members might "become empowered not only to imagine change but to actually practice that change, reflect collectively on the suggestion, and thereby become empowered to generate social action."[27]

HyeRan Kim-Cragg affirms the impact of a collaborative homiletic in her important book *Postcolonial Preaching:*

> Just as preaching should not be understood exclusively in terms of a verbal exercise, neither should it be understood as a solo endeavor. An appreciation of the role of the preacher as shared and owned by the whole community is essential. Preaching has no weight unless it is the corporate body of faith that lives by it. . . . Preaching as a theological body language uses the language of social relationships that is formed by the community.[28]

26. One of the ways the church has room to grow is to expand its cadre of preachers to include lay preachers. If preachers trust their congregation members to proclaim out in the world, why not in the sanctuary? While indeed singular "ownership" of the pulpit is being challenged, preachers still have the responsibility of "stewarding" the pulpit; this proposal is not an opportunity for the pastor to abandon preaching responsibilities altogether, especially since at their ordination they made promises to preach.

27. Doug Paterson, "A Brief Biography of Augusto Boal," Pedagogy and Theatre of the Oppressed, accessed March 30, 2021, https://ptoweb.org/aboutpto/a-brief-biography-of-augusto-boal/. Now active in more than seventy countries, Boal's Theatre of the Oppressed is "a format of theatre activities and performances that engages communities in social change." Communities are invited to be active participants in that change—first in a performance forum as a kind of rehearsal for the forum of life. Spectators have become "spect-actors" so that they might rehearse being agents of change in the world.

28. HyeRan Kim-Cragg, *Postcolonial Preaching: Creating a Ripple Effect* (Lanham, MD: Lexington Books, 2021), 90. Kim-Cragg reminds readers that "knowledge is perspectival and perspectives are power-laden" (110).

SUMMARY

As part of the liturgy, the sermon is the work of the people too. Change will be difficult. Film directors also know both the difficulty and the wisdom of this kind of collaboration.

> To take full advantage of the ideas and opinions of others, you need to be willing—at different times—to hold the reins and take over, while sometimes you will need to let them go and let yourself be guided. Stay open to the back and forth, as you learn to recognize when you need help and how to use it well.[29]

Examples abound of preachers who have made a shift in their preaching ministries in order to "stay open to the back and forth" of "holding the reins" and being guided by congregants. Perhaps just a few examples will suffice. A pastor from Laramie, Wyoming, noted:

> I am beyond excited with our [congregation's] preaching group. We have 7 members of our congregation [participating]. I only have one that is on the fence about preaching. . . . We have been meeting in between our gatherings and they have been going really well. We are doing Bible Studies on the lessons they will be preaching on in the coming months. We are currently working on a video to share with our congregation about what we are doing. This is a shift in our ministry so we wanted to make sure to share the vision.

A member sent the following note to the pastor who invited her to participate in the congregation's preaching ministry:

> Thank you, Pastor Brian! I realized the true purpose of "the people's sermon" or lay preaching through this experience. The past couple of weeks my focus and thoughts have been centered around these Gospel lessons on the Good Shepherd. Perhaps taking on the opportunity of writing a sermon is the only way a person such as myself can learn how not to be distracted and how to keep my attention on Jesus. This has been a great blessing!

29. Dorothy Fadiman and Tony Levelle, *Producing with Passion: Making Films That Change the World* (Studio City, CA: Michael Wiese Productions, 2008), 11.

A third example comes from a dissertation project focused on trauma-informed, collaborative preaching in the Indonesian context. Linna Gunawan received the following feedback after engaging in a very collaborative approach before, during, and after a sermon:

> This collaborative preaching is very rich [in meaning] . . . for me, [the sermon] became more realistic, both the content of the sermon itself and the method. The sermon, in essence, becomes richer, more realistic as more people give ideas and thoughts. We felt like God's Word was speaking directly to us. Especially when this model invites speakers who are experts in their fields, even invites people who have problems. Their involvement ultimately made this sermon very realistic because they were restored [by the Word, which was prepared together].[30]

It's time to broadcast the call for cast and crew. And then we can let the sermonic credits roll with a long list of collaborators, from the children in the fifth-grade Sunday school class to the adult Bible study participants to community elders to the Holy Spirit. As we progress through these chapters, think about whom you might cast for the various identified roles and responsibilities.

---

30. Experience shared by Duma Panggabean in Linna Gunawan, "Indonesian Collaborative Preaching for Collective Trauma Healing" (diss., Graduate Theological Union, 2003), 307.

3

Fade In: Creating the Opening

The beginning of a sermon sets in motion the sermon's theme and tone, the connection to the biblical story, the relationship between preacher and hearer, and more. In other words, the sermon opening is full of meaning as the entry point for the congregation. These first moments have been variously labeled as introduction, opening, the hook, beginning, orientation, or simply the first move. A preacher might choose a term based on its function. For example, an introduction seeks to present the sermon's main theme. A beginning is simply the starting point. A hook seeks to grab the listener's attention. While a film opening must work quickly to engage viewers using sights and sounds, characters and subjects in order to prevent them from tuning out or clicking elsewhere, since a preacher's audience is already sitting quietly in the pew waiting for the preacher to say something, "sermon beginnings are primarily not designed to gain attention."[1] Thus the potential effect of a sermon opening is far more expansive than the proverbial attention-seeking hook. The preferred term utilized in this book is "sermon opening" in order to align with the opening scene in filmmaking. So, what can openings do? And how? Filmmakers can assist preachers in answering these questions.

---

1. John C. Holbert and Alyce M. McKenzie, *What Not to Say: Avoiding the Common Mistakes That Can Sink Your Sermon* (Louisville, KY: Westminster John Knox Press, 2011), 36.

Just as the filmmaker has numerous options for an opening scene of a film, so does the preacher for an opening move of a sermon. Our goal here is for preachers to broaden their repertoire of possible sermon openings so that they can choose the kind of opening most likely to yield the overall desired effect of a sermon. Preachers can and should be as intentional about their sermon openings as filmmakers are about their opening scenes. This chapter identifies the myriad of choices filmmakers make to create an opening scene based on the role the scene plays to set up the rest of the film, and it provides concrete recommendations for making analogous choices about the preacher's opening move.

But first, let's focus on what you already do in those first moments. Before proceeding, take some time (even just fifteen minutes) to review and describe the openings of your recent sermons. Do you begin . . .

> . . . in the present or in the past?
>
> . . . with an announcement of the sermon's main theme?
>
> . . . with a thought-provoking question?
>
> . . . by describing an image vividly?
>
> . . . with a joke to "warm up the crowd"?
>
> . . . with something personal?
>
> . . . with a *MacGuffin* that won't appear at all later in the sermon?[2]

Note especially if you have a tendency to open all your sermons in the same way (e.g., with a contemporary story or a retelling of the biblical story just read).

Now take this exploration to a deeper level by articulating why you do what you do. What is the desired effect of what you do? Some preachers' primary hope in the beginning of the sermon is to capture the audience's attention. However, warming up the crowd with a funny story from the preacher's life in the past week or a joke that is utterly disconnected from the rest of the sermon is at best ineffective and at

---

2. "'MacGuffin' (a.k.a. McGuffin or maguffin) is a term for an object or element in a story that drives the plot, but serves no further purpose. It won't pop up again later, it won't explain the ending, and it won't do anything except possibly distract you while you try to figure out its significance." TV Tropes, s.v. "MacGuffin," accessed August 9, 2023, https://tvtropes.org/pmwiki/pmwiki.php/Main/MacGuffin.

worst in poor taste.[3] Such choices might actually point to the preacher's discomfort. Remember, the congregation has already been plenty "warmed up" with greetings, prayers, singing, and the reading of Scripture. They've stuck with the liturgy to this point, so, preacher, you've got their attention. Now say something that matters, at least something that connects to your subject.

Your goal should be to recognize what you do and why in the first minutes of your sermons. Take it from filmmakers who know that the opening scene of a movie is a precious opportunity to embed its character(s), setting(s), or subject matter on the audience's psyche.

Whether a film begins with a sock in the jaw (*Rocky*, 1976, and innumerable other fight films) or a kiss (*Just a Kiss*, 2002), its opening aspires to entice viewers to stick around and see what happens during the rest of the film. This enticement might appeal to viewers' desire for knowledge (e.g., a biopic or a cooking show) or escape (*Planet of the Apes* series), or it may ask them to suspend belief to go on a journey to, for example, the mythical Pandora (*Avatar* movies) or a mythological China (*Crouching Tiger, Hidden Dragon,* 2000), or to a mystery in modern-day New York City (*Only Murders in the Building* series). With its enticing appeal, a film's opening gives an inkling of what is to come, and it promises to deliver, thereby captivating the viewers sufficiently that they continue to watch.

Mise-en-Scène

Composed of a scene or a series of shots or scenes, a film's opening introduces its time, place, situation, point of view (POV), character(s), tone, genre, and/or theme and reveals the director's aesthetic in its *mise-en-scène.* Applied to filmmaking, mise-en-scène is the design of a scene's setting and elements—its actors, objects, props, lighting, spacing, costumes, and so on—and how they're positioned and move or are moved within a shot. Filmmakers place people in situations and invite the audience to see what transpires. Russian director and film theorist Andrei Tarkovsky writes in his book *Sculpting in Time,* "Juxtaposing

3. This point is not to suggest that humor has no place in sermons. See especially the book on humor in this series, *Humor Us! Preaching and the Power of the Comic Spirit* by Alyce McKenzie and Owen Hanley Lynch (Louisville, KY: Westminster John Knox Press, 2023).

a person with an environment that is boundless, collating him with a countless number of people passing by close to him and far away, relating a person to the whole world, that is the meaning of cinema."[4]

The mise-en-scène encompasses shot angle and composition as well as the scene's POV and atmosphere—in a nutshell, whatever is placed in front of the camera for the audience to absorb. Mise-en-scène requires collaboration with other departments, including set design, lighting, props, talent, and camera, but ultimately it reflects the director's style. It is part of what distinguishes a Hitchcock film from a Jane Campion or Wes Anderson film. David Thomson, referring to Hitchcock's *Rear Window* (1954), observes that the director "worked on the principle that everything we could see we would interpret" and that "the whole thing, the view, is a setup."[5] The opening of a film is its setup, a foreshadowing akin to the overture of a symphony. Indeed, a film opening is usually accompanied by music or sounds of some nature; it has an aural presence. It also has a POV provided by the eye of the camera. And it often starts *in medias res* (Latin for "in the middle of things")— in the middle of an action, such as a chase scene. In short—and a film's opening exposition is short, usually not much more than three minutes—a film's opening introduces the setting as it sets up the story.

An example of a masterful opening can be seen in *The Shape of Water* (2017), winner of an Academy Award for Best Picture and Best Director. It opens with a dream in which the apartment of the lead character, Elisa Esposito (Sally Hawkins), is underwater. As light music plays, a narrator tells an expository fairy tale *intercut* with dialogue from a Cleopatra-type movie running in the movie theater below.[6] Everything is watery blue as the camera moves down a hallway and through Elisa's apartment. We see small fish swimming and objects floating: chairs, an end table, and finally a couch with her sleep floating above it. This shot cuts to Elisa waking up and going through her morning ritual from her bed to her place of work. We absorb her rhythms and the time period (early 1960s) along with her living situation, class level, neighbors, and the fact that she's deaf and mute and communicates through sign language. We are intrigued by the underwater sequence and want to know how the story will connect her dream life with her

4. Andrei Tarkovsky, *Sculpting in Time* (Austin: University of Texas Press, 1985).

5. David Thomson, *How to Watch a Movie* (New York: Vintage Books, 2017), 65.

6. Intercutting is editing different images or sounds from different times and places within a scene.

daily life. The story is told from Elisa's POV; we see her and what she sees, and we want to know more.

See it for yourself! Watch the opening scene from a favorite movie or TV episode. Notice how the visuals and audio bring you into the world of the character(s). Where is the camera, and what is its focal length? Does it start with a wide shot, setting the geography, relative positions of the characters, time of day, time period, and weather? Or did the director choose a tighter (medium) shot of a character to place them in the environment or a close-up to highlight a detail or show a character reacting? Notice the POV along with the conflict, plot, theme, and genre. You'll likely need to watch a second time to take all this in.

You could also try viewing a scene with the sound turned off. Does silence make the camera and its moves and angles more apparent? Do you notice the edits? How were you brought into the world more fully or differently? Then try the reverse: leave the sound on and turn off the picture. How does this change your perception of the world of the film? What hooked you? Cognitive psychologists refer to this feeling of being transported to the world of the movie as *narrative transportation.* They have also discovered that "if we feel empathy and identify with characters, we become mentally attuned to the goals and intentions of those characters. Therefore, if a protagonist has a goal to find his or her child to prevent a death . . . it becomes our goal, too."[7]

Where to Enter the Story

Filmmakers strive to create the shortest, most efficient *exposition* possible. For filmmakers, exposition does not explain. Rather, it sets things up by showing, not telling, and is equivalent to a prologue in literature. Filmic exposition starts with a screenwriter who pens the opening and hopes it grabs and holds the potential buyer. After the screenplay is bought, polished, and finalized, the film is shot and edited and the expositional opening scene further perfected. Often a TV show will open with a *teaser,* a short scene that sets up the world and situation to draw in the audience. The miniseries *Love & Death* (2023), having established the 1970s world of Wylie, Texas, during

7. Anna-Lisa Cohen, "I'm Going to Spoil Your Favorite TV Show," *New York Times,* May 8, 2023, https://www.nytimes.com/2023/05/08/opinion/spoilers -succession-science.html.

opening credits and stating, "This is a true story," starts episode 1 with a pan through a suburban house. No one is home but when the camera reaches the laundry room, it teases elements of a bloody murder scene, then cuts to an overhead shot of a church with a choir singing overlaid with a subtitle, "Two years earlier." As it zooms into the church, we're hooked: we want to meet these people and find out who killed whom and why.

Commonly, as with *The Shape of Water*, the story begins and develops under head (opening) credits. *Parasite* (2016), another winner of the Academy Award for Best Picture, pulls the audience into a family's basement apartment and the predicament of their poverty. The split-screen head credits of *127 Hours* (2010) introduce the film's risk-taking protagonist as he leaves the city behind, driving through the night to set off on his fateful hike. Television series often use opening credits and the main title to place viewers in the show's world. *Mad Men* (2007–15) is a prime-time example. The show's animated head credits of a silhouetted man falling against a backdrop of billboarded skyscrapers evoke the world of advertising, the cool despair of the early 1960s, and the opening credits of Hitchcock's *North by Northwest* (1959).

Whether or not the action starts under credits, in designing exposition, an important decision for the screenwriter, and later for the director and the editor, is to figure out where to enter the story. Should it begin with two characters meeting, marrying, or divorcing? A film can start at or near the beginning of a character's life, as *The Aviator* (2004) does, with Howard Hughes as a boy being bathed by his mother and soaking in her germaphobe worldview.

In Medias Res

Most movies open in medias res because they start later in the main character's life, not with their birth, but in the middle or on the brink of a crisis or fomenting of a seminal event. For example, *Rocky* begins with Rocky in the middle of a fight, boxing badly. The original *Star Wars* film was actually the fourth in linear time; later movies in the series—prequels, in a sense—centered on what happened before, "a long time ago in a galaxy far, far away."

Movies also regularly start at the end of the story and work back to the beginning. *Pan's Labyrinth* (2002) begins and ends with a dying girl, showing how the abuse from her fiendish stepfather escalates along with her escape fantasies between these bookends. The

TV series *Breaking Bad* could have opened with scenes of the main character, Walter White, at his job and with his family. Instead, its first episode kicks off with a teaser, depicting a terrified Walter in his underpants careening through the desert in an RV, before cutting to opening titles and working its way back to reveal how he got there.

Sermons are like most films in that they typically begin in medias res. The whole homiletical endeavor is essentially entering an ongoing story—God's story—in medias res. Even more, because the sermon is typically not preached right away in worship, it is also in medias res liturgically speaking. The worship service, with its music, litanies, prayers, and Scripture readings, has already established the tone. The sermon opening, then, is most effective when it meets that tone. What if you were to consider the Scripture reading(s) the opening of the sermon as it sets the scene, introduces characters, stimulates emotion, and creates a tone? Take, for example, these closing lines of a Gospel reading from Matthew:

> "As the weeds are pulled up and burned in the fire, so it will be at the end of the age. The Son of Man will send out his angels, and they will weed out of his kingdom everything that causes sin and all who do evil. They will throw them into the blazing furnace, where there will be weeping and gnashing of teeth. Then the righteous will shine like the sun in the kingdom of their Father. Whoever has ears, let them hear." (Matt. 13:40–43 NIV)

If the next words out of the preacher's mouth are a chipper "Well, isn't it a beautiful day to be together" or "A priest, a rabbi, and a garbage collector walked into a bar . . . ," the experience is jarring. The preacher might instead begin by acknowledging the difficulty of hearing such threatening words, thereby remaining faithful to the occasion, to the genre, one might say.

Even with this acknowledgment that the preacher always begins in the middle of things, there are options. Consider the classic distinction between inductive and deductive preaching. Deductive preaching (1) begins with the claim about the biblical pericope that preachers conclude from their preparation and then (2) explains how they have gotten there and (3) proves why the conclusion is fair and faithful. Because this classic three-point deductive sermon is anathema to the narrativity of filmmaking, we will focus on the benefits of preaching more inductively.

Inductive preaching, in contrast, seeks to induce a conclusion made by the audience themselves by taking them on a journey. The sermon moves from particulars to generalities. Instead of offering a conclusive claim, the opening raises questions as it reveals setting, tone, characters, and conflict, creating anticipation in the hearers. Many, including most famously Fred Craddock, have argued that this kind of orientation to the journey set before us is satisfying:

> The [biblical] exegete does not become impatient and collapse the distance [between preacher and the text] too soon. Rushing from *then* to *now* interferes with honest listening. The sermon that is in a hurry to speak to us today can be heard as lacking confidence in Scripture's capacity to gain and hold attention and robs the sermon of anticipation by a lack of restraint or an unwillingness to delay in arriving at the point. As in much of life, anticipation is a major source of pleasure as well as a pre-condition of learning.[8]

Craddock recalls his early days of preaching deductively: "No wonder I was uncomfortable in the pulpit; my listeners had to accept my point without participating in the process of arriving at it. . . . The preacher who studies the sacred text and then converts it into sum-maries, explanations, and syllogisms has robbed the text of much of its power."[9]

Preaching inductively could still begin with identifying the "end" from the outset, just as a film's opening scene might very well be the last chronologically. Take, for example, the 2022 film *Spoiler Alert*. The title itself suggests that the end will be known. The opening scene presents Michael lying in a hospital bed alongside his husband, Kit, who is dying of cancer. We know the end, and yet we watch. Why? Now consider another story, that of two women making their way to a tomb the morning after burying their beloved only to find that the tomb is empty. We know the end, and yet we listen. Why? In both cases, while the story opens with the conclusion, the answers

---

8. Fred Craddock, introduction to *The Collected Sermons of Fred B. Craddock* (Louisville, KY: Westminster John Knox Press, 2011), xiv.

9. Craddock, *Collected Sermons*, xv.

to questions like "How did we get here?" and "Where do we go from here?" are slowly revealed, or induced.

Consider also the opening scene of the 2022 Oscar-nominated film *The Banshees of Inisherin*, with its gloriously perfect setting of an Irish island village. Even the greens are greener than green in this place where people are happily working, walking to their destinations, and smiling and waving to one another. This idyllic pleasantness is interrupted when Pádraic knocks on his buddy Colm's door so that they can set off to the village pub for their daily pint. The close-up shot of Colm, stubbornly hunkered in his home, suggests something is off. The dark tones of that image are all the more telling because of the contrast with the bright greens surrounding Pádraic's walk to Colm's seaside home. Our curiosity is piqued, and the central question has been established.

Now imagine, instead, an opening scene in which a narrator gives away the conclusion (spoiler alert!) that what we are about to see is a story of a friendship gone awry as a way to allegorize the Irish civil war. In the hands of a master filmmaker, this opening could work but would likely be far less satisfying. Instead, the film opening creates the nagging itch that will be satisfyingly scratched by film's end. Preachers, think of this suspense-satisfaction dynamic with the sermon as well since, as David Buttrick writes, "Destruction of suspense (the possibility of the unexpected) is positively unkind."[10] That is true in both filmmaking and preaching.

What's in the "Frame" (and Why)?

What is the very first thing you want hearers to see (!) as you begin your sermon? Even though preaching is an oral/aural art, you still "direct their eyes" by stimulating hearers' imagination. Really see the first shot—the establishing shot—that seeks to situate the viewer/hearer in time and place. In other words, imagine the mise-en-scène. Think like a filmmaker and stage the opening scene.

---

10. David Buttrick, *Homiletic: Moves and Structures* (Minneapolis: Fortress Press, 1987), 200. Additionally, Buttrick disputes the slogan "Tell them what you're going to do, do it, and then tell them what you've done" by calling it a "disaster." "Introductions should *not* give away the structure of the sermon ahead of time in a pedantic fashion" (85).

Deciding where the opening will place the hearers temporally and geographically is vital. Will it be in first-century Galilee or in the present where the congregation is gathered, or in some other time and place? Whatever your choice, consider that the tone should either be faithful to the biblical account(s) just read or have a very good reason for leaving the reading(s) behind (even if only momentarily). Let's say you decide to begin by taking the hearers into the world of the biblical story. Two of the film opening options noted above are especially useful here. Establish the setting by giving your hearers details about who is speaking to whom. Who else might be listening in? Tell us where the characters are geographically and temporally. Or you could forgo those details and zoom in on one particular character or perhaps the present dilemma. Maybe you'll want to zero in on the speaker who is clearly frustrated.

Now you must decide what will be included in the frame, essentially the mise-en-scène. Let's consider this decision specifically in terms of cinematic shot making since, as David Thomson says, "A film teaches us to see, and the shot is its mechanism."[11] Different types of shots affect the audience differently. As one author writes,

> A master craftsman [*sic*] knows how to create a specific shot, but a director knows why. Part of a director's required knowledge is to understand the technical properties of film and then employ them creatively to advance the story. Without the connection between content and technique, you are watching two disjointed parts; the result, more often than not, is a technical exercise. . . . The first part of the director's job is knowing what the audience should be feeling, and when. The second part is harnessing the tools to get them there.[12]

While there is a broad range of film shot choices for the purposes of opening sermons, we'll focus here on three regularly used shots: wide, medium, and close-up.

---

11. Thomson, *How to Watch a Movie*, 107.

12. Jennifer Van Sijll, *Cinematic Storytelling: The 100 Most Powerful Film Conventions Every Filmmaker Must Know* (Studio City, CA: Michael Wiese Productions, 2005), xii.

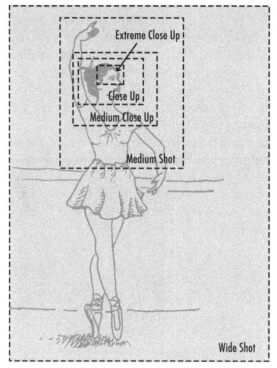

Figure 1 Illustration Courtesy of Jayne Weber

Wide Shot

The wide shot, often an extreme wide shot, sets up place, time, setting, and geography of people, objects, buildings, and so on. The opening of *The Banshees of Inisherin*, described above, is one example. Another is the opening of the documentary *Human Flow* (2017), in which the establishing shot of a vast body of water is so wide that it's disorienting. As the scene progresses, viewers begin to sense something moving. Suspense builds as viewers wonder what kind of boat they're seeing. An equivalent in preaching would be to offer the wider view of the biblical context. For example, "Picture with me the marketplace of first-century Jerusalem, situated at the crossroads of all corners of the world. Different products. Different languages. Different rules for living. The time was not for the faint of heart." Or, if you choose to begin in the present, a wide-shot sermon opening might offer something like, "Destruction is all around us. We see it. Even more, we feel it."

Medium Shot

The medium shot, considered the most used shot in filmmaking, zooms in to portray characters more prominently in the setting, typically showing them from the waist up. The opening scene of *Saving Private Ryan* (1998) is composed of mostly medium shots to center the film on the US soldiers and their emotions as they arrive at Omaha Beach on D-Day.

The medium shot is perhaps also most common in sermon openings. "Jesus had to get in his boat and pull away from shore." Or, to use a present-tense example, "Carol and Tanya had to wait twenty-five years to exchange their vows in front of us. But here they are. Here we are." More than the setting, the focus is on the characters and their relationships to one another.

Close-Up Shot

The close-up (CU) shot focuses tightly on a character, an important object, or a detail, and is also commonly used to open films. For example, *Citizen Kane* (1941) begins with a CU of a "no trespassing" sign on a chain link fence (outside Kane's Xanadu estate in Florida, where he is dying) before tilting up the fence. At 2:34 the scene contains two other CU shots: an extreme close-up of Kane's mouth uttering his last word, "Rosebud," and a CU of a snow globe with a midwestern house inside. The opening scene of *Back to the Future* (1985) zooms in on a collection of loud, ticking clocks on the wall. The viewer knows time will play a role in the film. The effect of the shot is to get the viewer to immediately wonder about and even fill in the gaps of the broader context.

One can imagine opening a sermon by describing the role of wine in first-century Cana or perhaps the vessel that holds such wine before zooming out to the story in which the wine or vessel plays a role. Or if the opening move of a sermon is set in the present, the preacher might begin with a close-up on the baptismal font before exploring the meaning of or biblical account of baptism: "The baptismal font is one of the most vital pieces of furniture in this room. Without it, this place would not be a sanctuary."

Already it is clear that the preacher has a range of choices when it comes to the sermon's opening move. All three shot choices are possibilities no matter what is in the frame, whether it portrays a landscape, object, or character. Let's take a closer look at how preachers might work with character.

Character Development

From the start, filmmakers want—no, need—their viewers to invest in the film's characters, be they heroes, sidekicks, or villains. One way to enter the story is by depicting characters and their dilemma, desires, traits, and so on. This option applies to sermon crafting, which ultimately wishes to present the Divine, whether that be a just Creator, a crucified and risen Christ, or a present and active Holy Spirit. Certainly, God is the protagonist for most, if not all, sermons. For the following examples, we will assume that sermons are biopics about God. Three elements from filmmaking can assist preachers when portraying God in their sermons: show, don't tell; POV; and focal length.

Show, Don't Tell

"Show, don't tell" is a filmmakers' creed. Meryl Streep's face alone can express more than a thousand words of dialogue. Since a camera can capture and captivate, filmmakers trust its moving images along with dialogue, music, sounds, and sound effects to tell the story. Opening scenes exemplify "show, don't tell," often through an economy of dialogue. Indeed, sometimes there are no words at all. The opening image of a movie embeds its character(s), setting(s), or subject matter in our psyche, usually hand in hand with music, narration, and/or sound effects. An image that zings and sings, as does the opening helicopter shot of Maria von Trapp (Julie Andrews) in *The Sound of Music* (1965), places us in the film's world and plants the movie in our minds. Other memorable opening images include these:

—*Apocalypse Now* (1979). The sound of helicopter blades grows over smoky blackness. Then a wide-screen shot of a tropical palm forest appears. Helicopters crisscross the screen, and yellow smoke rises from the bottom of the frame. The Doors song "The End" plays as the forest is napalmed and engulfed in flames. The opening immerses us in the war in Vietnam with a few penetrating visuals and sounds.

—*Sunset Boulevard* (1954). This noir film's flash-forward opening concludes with the body of screenwriter Joe Gillis (William Holden), who also narrates. The opening is effective because the audience is thrilled to be pulled into the world of Hollywood and immediately wants to know how Joe ended up face down in the pool.

—*The Deepest Breath* (2023). This documentary starts by showing free diver Alessia Zecchini as she dives many meters down into the ocean without oxygen. This opening effectively plunges us into her world with all its beauty—as seen in the light and darkness of the sea as she descends—and sets up the death-defying tension of pursuing this extreme sport.

The filmmakers' hoped-for effect of each of these openings is realized not just in terms of the movies themselves but because each opening stands out in our memories.

Similarly, preachers should avoid simply telling us what God does. Instead, show us. We come to know God through God's behavior, actions, reactions. In other words, show us who God is by describing what God does relative to God's beloved creations, including humans. The sermon opening is the primary place (primary in terms of both timing and importance) to begin.

POV and Focal Length

In choosing what hearers will see first, decide the opening's focal length (wide, medium, or close) and point of view (POV). Wherever you place the homiletical camera is where the hearers will be. Whatever the camera is pointing to is what they will see. Do we see the character (a kind of omniscient, third-person POV), or do we see what the character sees (first-person POV)? With the former, preachers can help hearers know God by explicitly casting God as the lead actor. In the latter, preachers focus more on the cast of characters presented in Scripture or the cast of characters who make up the present congregation.

Let's explore how these cinematic elements might be useful for preaching the story in John 4 of the Samaritan woman who meets Jesus at a well. Beginning with God as the subject at the opening of a sermon may be a less common choice, but it is a viable option since, in John 4, Jesus (who is God) is just as much a key figure as the Samaritan woman.

Jesus is tired. The trek from Judea to Galilee is not for the meek. He, too, has to rest. Somewhere in Samaria, around noon, he sits by a well. Perhaps he is exhausted emotionally as well. Word is spreading about Jesus the baptizer, but it's not always an accurate word. Even as Jesus is gaining in popularity he is gaining in notoriety.

While this opening could work, it tells a bit more than it shows. Here's another attempt:

Picture it: a windy, arid landscape in a desiccating noonday sun. Trees whip and swirls of grit provide the only action until we see something moving . . . a lone man wearily trekking through the dust. He reaches a well and sits on its edge. As the man stares into the opening, deep in the earth, a woman with a bucket approaches.

Notice how the latter option begins with a wide shot before moving in closer to a medium shot.

How would you focus on Jesus to open your sermon on John 4? You could choose to begin with an even wider shot or perhaps zoom in to a close-up. Any of the shot choices can work to orient the hearer for the sermonic journey ahead. Consider highlighting the actions, body language, and facial expressions that expose emotion without explicitly saying what they reveal. The Scripture reading itself provides much of the detail needed. But preachers can offer imaginative details faithful to the context to place hearers in the scene. Essentially, you become a screenwriter who must use just the right choice and number of words to describe the scene to potential directors.

Another option would be to focus on another character in the biblical story as a window into who God is, perhaps someone we do not usually hear from or know much about. Again, you can choose to present these characters using a wide shot, a medium shot, or a close-up. Consider these three examples, noting which of the options intrigues you the most and why.

Wide shot: The midday sun is burning at its hottest. No one dares to venture out of the shadows of the houses in Samaria. Down the street, a woman emerges from an alley and walks toward the well.

Choosing the wide shot sets the geography, relative positions of the characters, time of day, time period, and weather. While the character is in the frame, the focus is not yet fully on her.

Medium shot: As the sun's rays and rooster's crow awaken her from sleep, she tries to wrangle the usual stiffness from her joints.

This medium shot focuses more on the character in relation to their environment.

Close-up shot: The bucket swings with ease, revealing its emptiness. A hand with puckered skin clutches the rusty handle and moves with a determined rhythm.

Choosing the close-up presents a detail that is vital for what is to come. In this case, the listener is invited to get curious about the importance of the bucket and perhaps what is in it (or not in it).

Another option is to help hearers know God in a sermon opening by focusing on their life together as a congregation.

Your generosity this past year has helped our sister village in Africa drill three deep water wells. Recall John Smith's visit to our congregation last year. He reminded us of the significance of these wells, especially for the women who have spent practically their entire lives walking the many kilometers between their homes and fresh water. Two or three trips a day are necessary, since one trip isn't enough even to gather sufficient water for the evening meal.

Try This

Consider each of these examples as drafts of a sermon opening focused on character development that must then be filled out and honed. Choose one, revise it as you wish, and then explore the direction that takes the sermon.

How to Decide

Generally speaking, there is no right or wrong way to open sermons. But there are more and less effective openings for particular sermons dealing with particular topics offered on particular occasions. Likely, there will be multiple right elements (information, descriptions, actions) and multiple right shots (wide, medium, close-up) to include in the frame. Given the multitude of options, the choice for how to begin a sermon requires the deliberation and intentionality of a filmmaker who aims to capture the essence of the story, create a specific effect, and raise specific questions at the start of the film.

In the interest of making deliberate decisions concerning a sermon opening with maximum effect, consider the following questions. Start with the principal one: what is the central question or problem the sermon will address, and why should the hearers care?

The Central Question

Every film, whether it's a documentary, drama, or comedy, is, in a sense, a mystery: its opening leaves us with unanswered questions. For instance, the opening to *Breaking Bad* leaves us asking, "Why is Walter running scared for his life? Who is the dead guy in the passenger seat?" Beyond these questions is a central question that deals with the character's quest. Will they fail or succeed at overcoming the forces that oppose them? How? Even if the story is known, the plot is familiar, or the ending given, there is mystery in how the show will arrive at its conclusion. The opening has hooked us. We want to go along for the ride. We care about the character(s) or subject. We are primed to discover how the action will unfold. We want to keep watching even though we don't articulate our questions or know all the questions yet. We want answers. Thinking again about the opening of *The Shape of Water*, what central question do you think it raised? Perhaps "Who is the princess without a voice?"' and "What monster is trying to destroy everything?"

David Thomson, in a commentary on *Citizen Kane,* pushes the impact of a film opening beyond how it raises a question for the audience by considering the audience (spectator) to be a collaborator with the filmmakers:

> Every movie is not just a story, or a mystery, it is an information system in which things are revealed to us as the film thinks fit. . . . It is essential to this great film that [Orson] Welles wants the moment vivid, but mysterious, unsettling and fascinating. It's up to us. In other words, he has invited the spectator to be a part of his film as it begins. He's telling a story but he wants us to remember he's building a film, too, in which we must be active.[13]

When a film's opening does its job, we are entranced by vivid pictures and sounds and invited to keep watching, ask questions, and actively participate in the process of making meaning of the film as it progresses.

13. Thomson, *How to Watch a Movie,* 75.

The central question for the John 4 example might be: what does it say about God that Jesus dares meet this person as he does in this story, given the customs of the day around women and foreigners?

In addition, ask the following questions to help keep the focus on that central question:

—In what way is the Divine a protagonist in your sermon?
—Who are the other characters, and what is their relationship to God?
—What is the point of view? In other words, where is the camera?
—What is the focal length (shot choice) you are working with, and why?
—What is the desired effect of the opening move in the sermon?
—What tone is being established, and how?
—What world do you want to pull people into?
—Where is it?
—When is it taking place?
—What does it look, sound, smell, feel like?
—Toward what are you directing the hearers' mind's eye?
—What is the primary thing you want to reveal at this point?
—What are you planning to reveal later?
—How does this opening fit into the overall story or character development arc?
—Why is starting "here" necessary to get people "there"?
—What is the "there" you want to reach by sermon's end?
—Is there anything that is unnecessary?

Trial and Error

Crafting the sermon opening is a process of trial and error as you audition a variety of possibilities. If at all possible, connect with collaborators (members of your impact team) to test your sermon-opening possibilities. If team members' feedback matches your initial intent, chances are good that you are moving toward the right choice.

The opening may not be the first thing you wish to finalize. That is OK. Once you've created a full draft of the sermon, return to the opening to tweak (overhaul?) as needed. *A Beautiful Day in the Neighborhood* screenwriter Micah Fitzerman-Blue says, "It's super rare [to not have to change the opening]. Everything is usually so up for grabs. But we weren't easing the audience in. It's a microcosm of the movie, and hopefully it asks a lot of questions."[14]

Timing

Film openings have changed over the course of film history. *Farewell* (2019) director-writer Lulu Wang says,

> A lot of older films take more time to set up. . . . Modern audiences have become more sophisticated with visual language, and pick things up quickly. I wanted to establish the main relationship of the movie, the two different worlds they live in, and have audiences lean in and say, "This isn't what we expected." I was able to do all those things while simultaneously building character.[15]

The same is true with modern congregations who can pick up things about a sermon very quickly. Even with its many duties, the sermon opening works best when it does not linger. Just as holding the vast shot of the ocean too long (*Human Flow*) can lose viewers, going on too long about the arid landscape of Samaria can lose hearers' interest. Once the goal or desired effect of the opening scene has been accomplished, quickly move on. A commonplace rule of thumb is that a sermon opening should be fewer than fifty words. While such suggestions can be helpful for keeping the opening efficient, eventually preachers develop a feel for when it's time to move on. Even so, a checklist is useful. Ask yourself: Have I engaged the listener by:

14. Randee Dawn, "Screenwriters on Nailing That All-Important Opening Scene," *Variety,* January 3, 2020, https://variety.com/2020/film/awards/screen-writers-first-scene-lena-waithe-greta-gerwig-noah-baumbach-1203456297/.

15. Dawn, "Nailing That Opening Scene." David Thomson remarks on the increasing sophistication of film audiences: "It is as deliberate as the rectangle of our screen or frame remains firm. More than we may be able to articulate quickly, the patterns of this shot-making have entered our consciousness: . . . we are not surprised to hear the central logic of master shot and detailed close-ups that is used in filming countless scenes; we anticipate that shooting a character from the rear is likely to lead to some demon coming up behind them, goosing them or devouring them. We may not know the term 'offscreen space' (a critics' favorite) but we feel its potential as easily as we expect the unexpected in life" (*How to Watch a Movie*, 104).

- ✓ recognizing the desired effect of the opening
- ✓ setting the scene geographically
- ✓ setting the scene temporally
- ✓ introducing the main character(s)
- ✓ presenting the main theme
- ✓ setting the tone
- ✓ revealing what needs to be revealed
- ✓ refraining from revealing too much
- ✓ offering a clear point of view

SUMMARY

As the variety of film openings show us, there are countless ways to begin a story and more possibilities available to preachers than hooking the hearers with a silly joke or a disconnected contemporary story. The goal in this chapter has been to expand your repertoire of sermon openings so that you can mix it up for the hearers (and for you). Predictability has its place, but in the case of sermon openings, variety keeps hearers engaged. Honing this part of sermon crafting is worth time and effort because it is like a film's first scene, which "is the most valuable real estate a film has to offer."[16]

16. "Art of the Opening Scene—How to Start a Movie 6 Different Ways, from Nolan to Baumbach," Studio Binder, May 24, 2021, YouTube video, 14:59, https://www.youtube.com/watch?v=Jw_ysaoVlt4. In a 2020 *Variety* interview, writer-director Greta Gerwig reflected on scripting the "one piece [that] was more important than the others: the opening scene" of *Little Women* (2019). "Getting the opening just right was so important. When I had it, I thought, 'There's a movie here.' I knew I could make that movie."

Try This

Now it's time for you to put these ideas into practice. Return to the sermons you reviewed as you began this chapter. Choose one or two to amend according to the recommendations in this chapter.

1. Consider the Scripture reading(s) the opening that sets the scene, introduces a set of characters, stimulates emotion, creates a tone. Is there something from these options to choose as a starting point?
2. Revisit the biblical pericope of focus and identify its tone. Compare that tone to the tone of the sermon's opening. Do they correlate? If not, tweak the opening so that it matches the tone of the biblical story.
3. Remember that where one begins is typically not where one will end up. Consider the opening relative to the arc of where you want to take people.
4. If you begin with a contemporary story about yourself, rewrite to focus on a biblical character as the protagonist. Write it as if you were establishing the setting through a character's action in a screenplay.
5. Change the focal length or framing; for example, switch from a medium shot to an extreme close-up.
6. Take out all that is unnecessary and reshape only those elements that are necessary for what is to come in the sermon.

4

Scene, Beats, and Pacing: The Building Blocks

One doesn't set the camera at a certain angle just because the camera-man happens to be enthusiastic about that spot. The only thing that matters is whether the installation of the camera at a given angle is going to give the scene its maximum impact.
—Alfred Hitchcock[1]

THE IMPACT OF A SCENE

Mundanely, a *scene* can be described as a series of camera shots or a single shot that shows a narrative event and completes with a change in time, location, narrator, character, or action. Magically, a scene consists of and serves a whole lot more as it imprints in viewers' minds and is quoted, reenacted, and talked about as it ripples out of the screen and into the world.

In chapter 1, we looked at making an impact with films and preaching. In this chapter, we address how individual film scenes steal the show—that is, have impact. A film scene may impact us because it introduces a memorable character or contains dialogue that becomes etched in the culture, like "There's no place like home." The same could be said about any number of biblical scenes, such as the image of Jesus on the cross saying, "Father, forgive them, for they know not what they do."

Individual moviegoers are impacted by scenes that speak to them personally. They may see themselves in the scene or story and identify heavily with a character. The scene may align with their values or appear at a relevant time in their life or after a particular experience. Some scenes achieve impact by being cathartic, stretching viewers, or

1. Francois Truffaut, *Hitchcock* (New York: Simon & Schuster, 1966), 71.

stimulating their imagination and creativity. Others, such as pie throwing scenes, are just plain fun. While not too many biblical scenes have the same entertainment value as a pie-throwing scene, the other impacts noted here apply.

A scene's impact may be seen in its indelible images or special effects, like the *Star Wars* series' opening image of words disappearing into outer space. A scene can also achieve impact due to its time period—past or future. Many scenes in *Paris after Midnight* (2011) slipped viewers into bygone eras. Most Westerns place us instantly in the world of cattle and cactus, beginning with slow sweeps of the plains accompanied by sound effects or music and devoid of dialogue. After its opening scene, *Barbie* (2023) plants us in Barbie Land; *Asteroid City* (2023) anchors us in a fantasy 1950s desert—both with breathtaking pastels.

Scenes may reflect the social milieu (*Barbie*) or stimulate viewers because they flip the usual script with innovative storytelling (*Eternal Sunshine of the Spotless Mind,* 2004). Contrarily, many a scene gains its lasting appeal by being similar to other scenes and bringing comfort or a character's redemption. Horror scenes can be both impactful and iconic, as Hitchcock proved repeatedly. *Schindler's List* (1993) elicited both horror as Jews were forced to work in a Nazi factory and redemption as Schindler, the factory owner, also saved Jews from deportation and death. Last, a scene can impact viewers by taking them to other lands—real or fictional—to learn, grow, escape, or experience the extraordinary.

These examples are a few of the myriad ways scenes impact us and take us places we had not imagined. So, too, with sermonic scenes or moves, which can comfort and challenge, shock and sustain. The aim here is to explore *how* individual segments of sermons might utilize the acumen of filmmaking in order to, as Hitchcock said, "give the scene its maximum impact." We will start by identifying the crucial building blocks for how a film scene achieves impact.

Cinematic Scenes

What do you see when watching a scene in a film? In addition to the characters, there are many elements to absorb in each frame. There's the setting, the time of day, the lighting. The scene may have a blue, red, yellow, sepia, or natural cast created through filters and lighting to represent tone, time, or emotion. The scene will likely have physical objects—tables, chairs, trees—in the foreground and background. Unless it plays in a single shot, the scene will be composed of shots of different focal lengths (wide shots, medium, close-ups, etc.) and different angles (tilted, overhead, over the shoulder, etc.). You may also notice the *blocking* as characters move and interact with each other, advancing and receding in the frame. Viewers follow movement; blocking capitalizes on that to draw out the story and deepen its reach and meaning.

It takes numerous elements to put viewers in the world of a film and keep them fully engaged. We will now set about breaking down how these elements are brought together to construct scenes and build a film.

Scene Headings

The moviegoer experiences films as a whole in one sitting, but they are not constructed this way. After typing "FADE IN," the screenwriter writes a series of scenes that compose the screenplay and move it toward its conclusion and the final words, "FADE OUT" or "THE END." Every scene begins with a *scene heading* that states the scene's location and time of day, starting with whether it will be shot inside (interior, INT.) or outside (exterior, EXT.). For example: INT. NOTRE DAME—DAY. If the year or time period is important, it can be tacked on at the end: EXT. WAILING WALL — NIGHT — 70 BCE.

In addition to dialogue, voice-over dialogue, and short paragraphs of description defining a setting or character, a scene may contain a *slug line* or two to explain important actions or to reveal a detail about a character. Here's a sample of a scene with all five components: heading, description, dialogue, slug line, and VO dialogue.

```
FADE IN:
JULY 1957 LOWER EAST SIDE, BROOKLYN, NEW YORK
[heading]

EXT. ROCHLIN'S STATIONERY STORE AND FOUNTAIN
— DAY [heading]

Despite the "New Owners" sign, business is
slow. RO REILLY, 34, looks at the store and
apartment above it—the place that's been home
most of her life—one last time. [description]
```

HONNNNK! The horn brays from a middle-aged Nash parked in front. **[description]**

INT. NASH — DAY

ARTHUR REILLY, 36, lays on the horn. In the back seat DEBORAH REILLY, 12, with dark, tightly curled hair like her Jewish mother, and her brother BRIAN, 10, with straight, fair hair like his Irish Catholic father, fidget, impatient.

> DEBORAH **[dialogue]**
>
> C'mon, Ma!

Clutching a battered SEWING BOX of Old World—Russian—design, Ro steps into the front seat as if entering Sing Sing. **[slug line]**

Without a backward glance, Arthur guns the Nash, quickly putting the store and apartment behind them. **[slug line]**

> DEBORAH (VO) **[voice-over]**
>
> In 1957 Manifest Destiny called my family. We left Brooklyn and crossed the George Washington Bridge.

EXT. GEORGE WASHINGTON BRIDGE — DAY

Ro, jaw set, lights a cigarette. Arthur rolls down his window and sticks his head out, happy as a dog. Deborah and Brian peer excitedly through the girders, upriver, to the New Jersey Palisades. **[description]**

> DEBORAH **(VO)** (cont'd)
>
> We were going to start a new life in America's new frontier: suburbia.[2]

---

2. Gael Chandler, *Hide 'n Seek*, screenplay, 1.

Scene Structure and Type

There are multiple reasons for the order and placement of scenes. A scene may be prompted by the action in the scene before it, linked to an earlier scene, or contain important action or information that sets up the next scene. A scene can also appear to have no relation to what's happened thus far but make sense in terms of the story and what the audience needs to know at the moment. The order of a film's scenes may be linear or nonlinear and may change during editing. Scenes can be added, moved, flipped (reordered internally), split, trimmed down, or dropped entirely. Whatever happens to a scene in its journey from script to screen, it must contain a beginning, a middle, and an end. This imperative has century-old roots.

Following Russia's 1917 revolution, Soviet filmmakers founded the Moscow Film School, the world's first cinema college, in 1919. They pulled apart reels of American films to study their structure, shot their own films, and developed many lasting theories of filmmaking. One theory converted German philosopher G. W. F. Hegel's dialectic—thesis, antithesis, synthesis—into setup (beginning), conflict (middle), and resolution (end) as the three necessary components of a scene. Here's a straightforward example from the final scene in *The Wizard of Oz* (1939) that takes place in Oz:

> **Beginning (setup):** The wizard leaves in a balloon without Dorothy after Toto scurries off and she hops out of the basket to retrieve him. Having missed her chance to return home to Kansas, she's dejected and her pals console her.
>
> **Middle (conflict):** Celestial Glinda touches down and tells Dorothy she's had the power to return home all along.
>
> **End (resolution):** Dorothy says goodbye to her three pals, clicks her heels three times, and departs Oz.

This is a *dialogue scene,* meaning a scene where people mainly talk to one another. The impact of dialogue scenes is seen as the audience meshes with the film's characters, absorbing their conflicts, reactions, relationships, and words and caring about what happens to them.

Other types of scenes also have a beginning, middle, and end. Here's an *action scene* from the same movie:

> **Beginning (setup):** A cyclone menaces the Kansas countryside and the family farmhouse, separating Dorothy from her family.

She enters the house, searching for them, yelling "Auntie Em" when a window knocks her out.

Middle (conflict): As her house spins in the twister, Dorothy comes to consciousness and looks out her bedroom window. People and animals of her Kansas world pass by as in a dream. Sound effects match the action while musical riffs (Munchkin theme and Witch theme) as well as the visual of Miss Gulch morphing into the Wicked Witch *foreshadow* Oz. The swirl of images ends and the sounds stop as the house crashes to the ground.

End (resolution): In silence Dorothy walks through the house and opens the door to the colorful land of the Munchkins and strains of "Somewhere over the Rainbow."

This scene not only transports Dorothy from Kansas to Oz but also transports the moviegoer from black-and-white to Technicolor. An action scene works best when it does not just show the car chase but also includes characters' reactions, thereby strengthening audience engagement and impact. Action scenes are those sensory "edge of the seat" scenes that physically impact viewers as they become immersed in spectacles that range from exhilarating to gut wrenching. Both action and dialogue scenes bring a change in time, location, narrator, character, or action and move the story forward by spurring events and characters' actions in the next scene.

The third type of scene, a *montage scene,* functions differently. Akin to a musical interlude and consisting of a mélange of images, a montage scene conveys facts, feelings, or thoughts that usually take the story along with the audience from one time or place to another. A montage typically has little or no *sync* dialogue and normally is accompanied by music or occasionally by non-sync sounds. A montage functions in four ways. First, it can be transitional, occurring between scenes or within a scene, like the middle part of the "twister" scene that takes Dorothy from Kansas to Oz (described above) accompanied by sound effects, musical riffs, and some short dialogue. Second, a montage can be expository, such as the three-minute pretitle sequence at the start of Spike Lee's documentary *When the Levees Broke: A Requiem in Four Acts* (2006–7). Set to jazz, this opening montage scene succinctly sets up the miniseries by intercutting the racial history of New Orleans and the devastation of the Ninth Ward by Hurricane Katrina in 2005. The transitional and expository montages impact the audience cerebrally or viscerally. A third type of montage scene functions as much-needed rest (akin to a musical rest) after a chaotic or violent action or dialogue scene, allowing the audience time to absorb, breathe, and recover. A superb example is the montage of kissing couples from old black-and-white movies following the funeral of a main character near the end of *Cinema Paradiso* (1988), which underscores it being a love story of films. Fourth, a montage may conclude a movie or TV series, serving as an epilogue and showing what happened to all the characters. as the prolonged montage in the finale of *Six Feet Under* does, or connecting past to present as *BlacKkKlansman* (2018) does when it ties a fictional story set in 1972 to the "Unite the Right" events of August 2017 in Charlottesville.

Beats

Just as scenes compose the stepping-stones of the screenplay and exhibited film, *beats*—the small shifts in action, emotion, thought, or tone within a scene—constitute the subtle change points within each scene. Actors, directors, screenwriters, composers, music editors, picture editors, and sound editors think in beats to aid in breaking a scene into manageable parts. Many shows create a *beat sheet* to outline the script. A beat sheet identifies the film's critical plot points and events using specific beats, such as the opening image, introduction, midpoint, low point, climax, resolution, and ending. A beat sheet can be a bulleted outline, a spreadsheet, or a table; it has no specific format. Here's a beat sheet for the action scene in which Dorothy (D) travels by house to Oz in the *Wizard of Oz*.

Key

FX=Hard (specific) sound effect; **BG**=Background sound effect; **MX**=Music; **DIAL**=Dialogue

Beat	Sound	Music
1) BLACK & WHITE film, D enters house as a chair crashes.	BG: cyclone/wind FX: chair crash	None
2) D walks through house to bedroom. D screams as a window knocks her out.	BG: cyclone/wind DIAL: "Auntie Em" FX: window crash DIAL: "Oh!"	MX begins: Warning MX

continued on next page

Beat (cont.)	Sound (cont.)	Music (cont.)
3) D on bed, unconscious. Superimpose spinning house and cyclone.	BG: cyclone/wind	Unconscious MX (horns & other instruments)
4) Begin stream of images through window (*matte shots*).	BG: cyclone/wind	Upbeat MX
5) D comes to and views the cyclone through the window. Sees Miss Gulch on a bike, then on a broom. (End stream of images.)	BG: cyclone/wind FX: animal sounds DIAL: "We must be inside the cyclone." DIAL: "Oh, Miss Gulch!" DIAL: Scream	Upbeat MX Munchkin theme Miss Gulch/Witch theme
6) House falls.	BG: cyclone/wind DIAL: Witch cackles DIAL: D screams	Active, big.
7) House lands.	FX: crash	MX stops.
8) D walks through house and exits.	Silence except for FX: door opens	
9) D opens door to COLOR film and Munchkinland.	BG: birds	"Somewhere over the Rainbow"

Visual and sound beats make up the *rhythm* (pacing) of a scene just as scenes and sequences compose the rhythm of the entire film. Pacing, along with time, influences the coherence and integrity of a film as well as how much time an audience is willing to invest in it. Hence filmmakers concentrate on pacing and time from the production (shooting) phase through the postproduction (editing) phase.

Pacing and Time

The great thing about the movies is . . . you're giving people . . . tiny pieces of time . . . that they never forget.

—Jimmy Stewart

Initially, the actors and camera create the pace of each shot; the actors with the pacing of their lines and actions, the camera with the film's *frame rate* (*slo mo*, real time, or *speedup*) and the pacing of the shots, such as a quick *pan* or a slow *tilt*. The editor works with *dailies* to then set the pace of the show, altering the real-time pace of the shots created during production. (See chap. 5 for more on editing and pacing.)

Filmmakers manipulate, er, finesse time to send a character (along with the audience) back in time via a *flashback* scene or forward in time via a flash-forward scene. These two narrative devices put the audience inside a character's mind to reveal their thoughts and feelings. Film is considered to be the art that most mimics the workings of the human mind because the audience experiences time subjectively from the character's point of view, darting from thought to feeling, knowledge to discovery, past to present in a matter of seconds or frames. Russian filmmaker Andrei Tarkovsky writes, "Unlike all the other art forms, film is able to seize and render the passage of time, to stop it, almost to possess it in infinity. I'd say that film is the sculpting of time."[3]

A flashback scene illuminates a character's memories as they rerun an earlier life event. Flashbacks are often used—and overused—as exposition, but they can also work to foreshadow the future, clarify plot points, or spin the story in a new direction. They can be quick—composed of a *flash cut* or two—or long, even running the length of the movie. The ending of *Pan's Labyrinth* (2006) reveals that the entire movie has been the flashback of a dying girl. Flashbacks may contain other flashbacks and occur in nonchronological order. Filmmakers deploy a flash-forward scene to presage upcoming events or disclose parts of the story that have not yet been told but will be picked up later in greater detail. An oft-seen example is a TV show's opening that begins with a character in danger and includes a caption like "twenty-four hours earlier." A flash-forward can bare a character's hopes and fears and frequently (as with a flashback) appears as a dream or nightmare.

No matter how a flashback or flash-forward scene functions, it is vital that as it sends the story backward or forward in time, it drives the story forward.

3. Andrei Tarkovsky, *Sculpting in Time: Reflections on the Cinema* (Austin: University of Texas Press, 1985).

Character Development

Just as scenes develop, characters develop. In fact, it's a bit of a chicken-and-egg situation: scenes develop characters and the development of characters makes scenes work. Viewers engage with characters and immerse themselves in their lives and fates. If they fail to do this, the film will flame out. So character development is a critical task for a filmmaker.

Whether the show is fiction or documentary or the scene is a dialogue scene, an action scene, or a people-filled montage scene, building the *arc*—the growth and movement—of each character or doc interviewee is crucial. Building the arc begins with the scriptwriter, whose creation is then interpreted by the actor. Next the character is blocked (positioned on the set), watched over, and melded with the other characters and the story by the director. Finally, the editor crafts the arc so that the audience lives and breathes with the character.

Characters can be animals—a dog or a Cowardly Lion, for instance. They may also be inanimate objects such as Dorothy's house or the cyclone. Christopher Boyes, sound designer on *Titanic,* said, "I love the way the groans accompany the slowly sinking ship that make you feel as if this incredible creation is resisting death—as if Titanic is a huge dying creature that's not giving up on life yet."[4] Nonhuman characters have a role to play and may even have a special melody (remember that shark in *Jaws*) or a sound effect like R2D2.[5]

Filmmakers ensure that each character or group of characters is integral to the film's narrative. With each scene, a filmmaker may ask, "Whose scene is this?" Usually the scene belongs to the main character or to the character with the most lines. It may belong to the character who listens and reacts. Why? Because in the next scene this character may do something important. Perhaps the workers quietly listening to the wage-cutting boss will go on strike in the next scene or the child being silenced will speak out.

How do filmmakers deal with problem characters, or should we say, problems with characters? If a character is not working, filmmakers drill down to find the answers. Here are a few examples:

4. Rachel Igel, "Interview with Christopher Boyes, Sound Designer, Titanic," Editors Net, 1997.

5. George Lucas named the character after the abbreviated label on a reel of sound effects: Reel 2, Dialogue 2. https://www.lucasfilm.com/news/history-in-objects-reel-2-dialog-2/.

1. Is the character poorly defined? Is the character important?

—Solution 1: Eliminate the character if it is unimportant or combine the character with another character if there are too many. Save the character for another show if it is bogging down this show.

—Solution 2: If the character is important, then it needs to be better defined or beefed up if it isn't seen enough. The audience must get to know the character and fathom its desires and motivations. They need to see the character's inner turmoil and outward reactions as it deals with the obstacles thrown at it. Showing its environment (home, living situation, companions, important possessions, occupation, preoccupations, etc.) may better define the character, as can infusing a bit of its *backstory* to help understand its compulsions. Note: It doesn't matter that audience members like a character, but it is critical that they care for a character. Hero, villain, sidekick, or supporting character, viewers must care about them and what happens to them. Chris Innis and Robert Murawski, coeditors on *The Hurt Locker* (2008), believe: "If audiences care about the characters, then they will be willing to submit to almost any film structure or rhythm."[6]

2. Is each character's arc clear? Do they evolve too quickly or too slowly?

—Solution: Rearrange scenes so that you are releasing character information at just the right pace. The audience must experience characters' growth or refusal to grow leading to their success, newfound wisdom, or downfall at a believable rate.

3. Does the character have too much backstory?

—Solution 1: Be merciless. Eliminate all backstory that is unnecessary or bogs down the story.

---

6. Gael Chandler refers to Rudy Koppl's article "The Hurt Locker: Blurring the Lines between Sound and Score" (2009) in *Music from the Movies Magazine.* See Chandler, *Editing for Directors: A Guide for Creative Collaboration* (Studio City, CA: Michael Wiese Productions, 2021), 149.

— Solution 2: Reveal the backstory at a better, more story-forwarding moment.

— Solution 3: Trickle it in over the course of the show to deepen the audience's understanding of the character and motivate the action.

Example: In early *Star Wars* (1977) edits, Luke Skywalker had too much backstory. He was introduced hanging out in the desert with a friend (an unimportant character), interrupting the initial battle scene where Princess Leia is captured. As reedited, Luke's entrance is integrated with haggling for two critical characters— droids C-3PO and R2D2—making all three characters and the action flow forward.[7]

Having identified the building blocks of a film scene and how best to maximize their impact, we turn now to how effective preachers might utilize these building blocks for impactful scenes in their sermons.

Sermonic Scenes

Preachers may not think of their sermons as containing scenes, but they certainly do aim to "put viewers in a world," which is the goal of a film scene. What follows are some homiletic practices that are useful for inviting people into a world, whether that be the biblical world or a possible alternative world in the present or future.

In her book *Making a Scene in the Pulpit*, Alyce McKenzie writes, "Scenes in a sermon can function, as they often do in literature and film, as ethical simulation chambers for dealing with real-life challenges, drawing us in to identify with characters, undergo changes with them, and take that changed perspective back into our world."[8] A scene as defined by McKenzie is simply a "small segment of a larger story." Preachers are accustomed to thinking in small segments. For example, the preacher's foundational text is usually a small segment of Scripture that is a part of a larger story. Even more, preachers often remind listeners that our lives are a small but significant segment of God's larger

---

7. Paul Hirsch, *A Long Time Ago in a Cutting Room Far, Far Away . . .* (Chicago: Chicago Review Press, 2019), 95–96.

8. Alyce M. McKenzie, *Making a Scene in the Pulpit: Vivid Preaching for Visual Listeners* (Louisville, KY: Westminster John Knox Press, 2018), 3.

story. In other words, the scene, understood as a part of a whole, has everything to do with preaching.

Working with Scenes in Scripture

In order to create and sequence segments (scenes) of a sermon that invite people into a world, preachers first work with scenes in Scripture. This section recommends three concrete sermon preparation practices that utilize the wisdom of filmmaking:

—Script the biblical scene.
—Describe the scene as if you were a filmmaker.
—Identify the scene's beats.

Script the Biblical Scene

First, "reformat" the biblical scene so that it looks like a script. Using John 18:33–40 as an example, the progression might look something like this, starting with what we usually see:

> [33]Then Pilate entered the headquarters again, summoned Jesus, and asked him, "Are you the King of the Jews?" [34]Jesus answered, "Do you ask this on your own, or did others tell you about me?" [35]Pilate replied, "I am not a Jew, am I? Your own nation and the chief priests have handed you over to me. What have you done?" [36]Jesus answered, "My kingdom does not belong to this world. If my kingdom belonged to this world, my followers would be fighting to keep me from being handed over to the Jews. But as it is, my kingdom is not from here." [37]Pilate asked him, "So you are a king?" Jesus answered, "You say that I am a king. For this I was born, and for this I came into the world, to testify to the truth. Everyone who belongs to the truth listens to my voice." [38]Pilate asked him, "What is truth?" After he had said this, he went out to the Jews again and told them, "I find no case against him. [39]But you have a custom that I release someone for you at the Passover. Do you want me to release for you the King of the Jews?" [40]They shouted in reply, "Not this man but Barabbas!" Now Barabbas was a rebel. (NRSVue)

As a first step, remove the verse numbers, which tend to obstruct a more narrative reading. While the numbers can be helpful for reference, they are unhelpful for getting readers into the story. (Verse and chapter indicators are add-ons—there is nothing sacred about them.) See what the same block of text looks like when presented in a more literary form:

> Then Pilate entered the headquarters again, summoned Jesus, and asked him, "Are you the King of the Jews?"
>
> Jesus answered, "Do you ask this on your own, or did others tell you about me?"
>
> Pilate replied, "I am not a Jew, am I? Your own nation and the chief priests have handed you over to me. What have you done?"
>
> Jesus answered, "My kingdom does not belong to this world. If my kingdom belonged to this world, my followers would be fighting to keep me from being handed over to the Jews. But as it is, my kingdom is not from here."
>
> Pilate asked him, "So you are a king?"
>
> Jesus answered, "You say that I am a king. For this I was born, and for this I came into the world, to testify to the truth. Everyone who belongs to the truth listens to my voice."
>
> Pilate asked him, "What is truth?"
>
> After he had said this, he went out to the Jews again and told them, "I find no case against him. But you have a custom that I release someone for you at the Passover. Do you want me to release for you the King of the Jews?"
>
> They shouted in reply, "Not this man but Barabbas!" Now Barabbas was a rebel.

Already the words "read" differently. Do you notice anything new in the story when it is offered in this format? As a reminder, no words or ordering of words are changed; only the layout has changed.

Now change these scenes into screenplay format. Screenplays follow strict style guidelines. They must always be in twelve-point Courier font. Whenever a scene changes, there is a scene heading written in "all caps." The purpose of this has to do, in part, with efficiency during the production in order to quickly understand the world we are being drawn into. Characters' names are written in all caps, with dialogue centered throughout the script. While these conventions may seem unnecessary for preachers, they will help us see the biblical scene in a new way.

JOHN 18:33-40

INT. PILATE'S HEADQUARTERS — EARLY MORNING
[**heading**]

PILATE enters and summons JESUS. [**slug line**]

> PILATE
>
> Are you the King of the Jews? [**dialogue**]

> JESUS
>
> Do you ask this on your own, or did others tell you about me?

> PILATE
>
> I am not a Jew, am I? Your own nation and the chief priests have handed you over to me. What have you done?

> JESUS
>
> My kingdom does not belong to this world. If my kingdom belonged to this world, my followers would be fighting to keep me from being handed over to the Jews. But as it is, my kingdom is not from here.

> PILATE
>
> So, you are a king?

> JESUS
>
> You say that I am a king. For this I was born, and for this I came into the world, to testify to the truth. Everyone who belongs to the truth listens to my voice.

> PILATE
>
> What is truth?

EXT. PILATE'S HEADQUARTERS — EARLY MORNING

       PILATE

  I find no case against him. But you have
  a custom that I release someone for
  you at the Passover. Do you want me to
  release for you the King of the Jews?

       CROWD

      (shouting)

 Not this man but Barabbas!

  What do you notice or discover by engaging the scene using a script format? The benefits of this process are many. First, by slowing down and engaging the scene in this creative way, the preacher begins to really see the scene. Even more, seeing something in a new way *on* the page yields new perspectives *off* the page.

Describe the Scene as if You Were a Filmmaker

Of course, the preacher's challenge is to stay faithful to the biblical account, lest one be accused of engaging in eisegesis. And yet, for preachers whose homiletical foundation is Scripture, the process requires interpreting the Bible for a new time and place, much as an adapted screenplay requires a screenwriter to rework an existing story for cinema. The goal is for the audience to visualize the story—to run it in their heads and experience its sights, sounds, and emotions. Therefore a next-level iteration may take some liberties by adding character descriptions; identifying slug lines that describe important actions, motivations, or details about a character's presentation; and offering slight changes in dialogue. The question, ultimately, is whether such liberties are faithful to the interpretive and proclamatory tasks. For now, freely explore more vivid details of the scene as if you were a screenwriter.

  Read the scene below (with some liberties taken for cinematic effect) and see how it plays in your mind and heart.

JOHN 18:33-40

INT. PILATE'S HEADQUARTERS — EARLY MORNING

PONTIUS PILATE, a judge of military bearing, enters and takes his throne, his robes askew and his mood provoked.

PILATE signals TWO GUARDS who lead Jesus in.

PILATE
(on his throne)
Are you the King of the Jews?

JESUS
Why do you ask? Who says this?

PILATE
Your own nation and the chief priests who brought you here. What have you done?

JESUS
My kingdom is not of this world. If it was, my followers would fight to keep me from you.

PILATE
So, you are a king?

JESUS
For this I was born: To testify to the truth. Everyone who belongs to the truth listens to me.

The two men eye each other as Pontius Pilate contemplates Jesus's words.

PILATE
What is truth?

```
EXT. PILATE'S HEADQUARTERS — EARLY MORNING
PILATE emerges and addresses the CROWD.

                    PILATE
     I find no case against Jesus. But you
     require that I release someone every
     year at Passover. Do you want me to
     release him, the King of the Jews?

                    CROWD
     NO! Not him. He's no king. Barabbas!
```

Preachers, like filmmakers, would do well to aim to "create experiences rather than report them."[9] To add more vivid detail to your sermonic scenes, we encourage you to describe every detail of a biblical scene as if you are adopting the various roles of a filmmaker. Describing the following will assist you:

1. Time of day or night (gaffer, person in charge of lighting)
2. Scenery and props (production designer)
3. What the camera is focusing on, from what angle, and at what distance (director of photography)
4. The characters' appearance—their body language, movement/blocking, expressions, voice when speaking (actor)
5. Sounds in addition to dialogue; ambience, musical track, sound effects (sound designer)

Paint a picture of what we will see and hear and how the sounds and visuals will impact us. When you really imagine what is in the scene, you will preach more vividly and your hearers will experience the world more clearly.

While this exercise might end up being only presermon work, it could actually become a segment in your sermon. In a sermon on Luke 14:15–24, Tom Troeger uses cinematic direction to set the scene for his hearers:

> As Luke's cinematic epic begins
> we see across the wide screen

9. McKenzie, *Making a Scene*, 2.

in elegant gold letters,
the title:
An Unforgettable Dinner Party.
The credits fade
and the camera starts with a wide shot
of sumptuous formal gardens
with a huge and elegant mansion
in the background.
We hear the bright voices of a woman
and a man talking on a veranda.
The camera pulls them into our vision.[10]

In another section of the sermon, Troeger elicits a montage (recall that a montage consists of a mélange of images that usually take viewers from one time or place to another):

And now there follows
scene on scene,
one quick image
after another of
chauffeur after chauffeur
being turned down.[11]

Thinking like a film director giving directions to their crew is a way to "engage the congregation in the story by activating their own imaginations."[12] Even though a preacher is typically not showing the scene on a screen, there is a way to use words to fulfill the recommendation: show, don't tell. Instead of just reporting things to the congregation, preachers "invite [them] somewhere (setting) to identify with someone (character)."[13] This point is especially important relative to character development. Take, for example, a line from the Troeger sermon above: "We hear the bright voices of a woman and a man talking on a veranda." If we want to depict more about each of these characters, we might describe their mood or their relationship to one another; for example, that they are never happier than when they are talking on the veranda. Or, perhaps, we use dialogue. The woman says, "I am never happier than when I'm talking with you like this."

10. Thomas Troeger, "Write the Sermon as a Movie Script," in *Ten Strategies for Preaching in a Multimedia Culture* (Nashville: Abingdon, 1996), 50.

11. Troeger, "Sermon as Movie Script," 53.

12. Troeger, "Sermon as Movie Script," 48.

13. McKenzie, *Making a Scene*, 2.

While that is a good start, it is still more telling than showing. Instead, avoid being the omniscient narrator telling us about your cast of characters or even having them describe their own feelings. Instead, show us: "The woman's smile puts the man at ease" and "His tensely downturned lips begin to soften until the edges ascend into a smile." McKenzie quotes writer Janet Burroway, "Simply labeling a character's emotion as love or hatred will have little effect; rather, emotion is the body's physical reaction to information the senses receive."[14] In this case, a smile and tense lips softening are the body's physical reaction that reveals emotion. The challenge in the movie industry is to "replace dialogue with visually innovative and engaging beats that use blocking, props, and your character's clever interaction with their environment."[15] So, too, in preaching.

Identify the Scene's Beats

Another way to "slice" the biblical scene is to identify its beats. Recall that beats are small shifts in action, emotion, thought, or tone within a scene; they constitute the subtle change in plot points within each scene. A beat sheet of the John 18 scene might include these beats:

— Pilate enters headquarters and summons Jesus.
— Pilate asks Jesus again about his royal identity.
— Jesus answers with a question.
— Pilate reiterates to Jesus how he's been betrayed.
— Jesus distinguishes his kind of kingdom.
— Pilate interprets this as Jesus's saying he is a king.
— Jesus turns it back on Pilate and philosophizes about truth.
— Pilate returns to the crowd outside and says he does not find Jesus guilty.
— Pilate inquires about releasing Jesus, which is the custom at Passover.
— The crowd doubles down on their betrayal by encouraging him to release Barabbas.

Notice, however, that much of this example is essentially describing lines of dialogue. Perhaps building on this starter beat sheet would be more useful.

14. Janet Burroway, *Imaginative Writing: The Elements of Craft*, 4th ed. (London: Pearson, 2014), quoted in McKenzie, *Making a Scene*, 101.

15. Jim Mercurio, *The Craft of Scene Writing: Beat by Beat to a Better Script* (Fresno, CA: Quill Driver Books, 2019), 63.

Key

FX=Hard (specific) sound effect; **BG**=Background sound effect,
MX=Music; **DIAL**=Dialogue

Beat	Sound	Music
1) Pilate (P) enters headquarters and summons Jesus (J).	BG: crowd yelling FX: shuffling of feet	None
2) P and J have an exchange about Jesus's so-called royal identity, betrayal, and kingdoms.	BG: muffled crowd sounds FX: door closes and echoes DIAL: (P) Are you the King of the Jews? (J) Do you ask this on your own, or did others tell you about me? (P) I am not a Jew, am I? Your own nation and the chief priests have handed you over to me. What have you done?	None
3) P seems to be trapping J, so J turns it back onto Pilate before philosophizing about truth.	BG: ambience DIAL: (J) My kingdom is not from this world. If my kingdom were from this world, my followers would be fighting to keep me from being handed over to the Jews. But as it is, my kingdom is not from here. (P) So, you are a king? (J) You say that I am a king. For this I was born, and for this I came into the world, to testify to the truth. Everyone who belongs to the truth listens to my voice. (P) What is truth?	None

continued on next page

Beat (cont.)	Sound (cont.)	Music (cont.)
4) Pilate returns to the crowd outside and says he does not find Jesus guilty.	BG: crowd yelling DIAL: (P) I find no case against him.	MX begins: Minor-key sounds indicating doom
5) Pilate inquires about releasing Jesus, which is the custom at Passover.	BG: crowd yelling DIAL: (P) But you have a custom that I release someone for you at Passover. Do you want me to release for you the King of the Jews?	MX: Builds in volume and intensity
6) The crowd doubles down on their betrayal by encouraging him to release Barabbas.	BG: crowd chanting DIAL: (crowd) Not this man, but Barabbas!	None

Notice the emphasis on the action. The building tension keeps us engaged.

This section of Scripture is really two scenes: one within the headquarters that contains dialogue between Pilate and Jesus, and another outside featuring the exchange between Pilate and the crowd. Each of the scenes has a beginning, middle, and end.

SCENE 1

Beginning (setup)	Pilate enters headquarters and summons Jesus.
Middle (conflict)	Pilate and Jesus dialogue.
End (resolution)	Pilate exits.

SCENE 2

Beginning (setup)	Pilate exits headquarters and addresses the crowd.
Middle (conflict)	Pilate declares Jesus's innocence and the crowd insists on Jesus's guilt.
End (resolution)	Pilate acquiesces to the crowd's guilty verdict.

Not all parts of the Bible are narrative scenes (psalms, letters, apocalyptic visions are among the exceptions). Whether their basis is narrative or nonnarrative, sermons can utilize the elements of scenes.

Try This

Try your hand at (1) creating a beat sheet of a different biblical scene and (2) identifying a scene's beginning, middle, and end.

Working with Scenes in the Sermon

Pacing and Time

There is an acute emphasis on time both within each scene as well as from one scene to the next. Indeed, the cinematic artist can manipulate or finesse time for impact. So, too, must the preacher, since we are not aiming for a static experience. Twentieth-century homiletician H. Grady Davis insists that "if we wish to learn from other arts, we must learn from these arts based on a time sequence."[16] Sermons are more akin to the "temporal arts," like filmmaking. As Eugene Lowry notes in his book *The Homiletical Beat*, "The primary medium of preaching is time, moving moment-by-moment."[17]

The congregation, like the moviegoer, experiences the presentation as a whole in one sitting. However, like a film, sermons are not constructed this way. Both films and sermons are built, crafted, or constructed step-by-step, scene-by-scene, beat-by-beat. Sermons move from one setting (Jerusalem, a street corner in Berkeley, or the sanctuary) or time frame (first century, 2020, or now) to another. This movement can be seamless, carrying the hearers along with them and offering audible cues for listening along the way. Sometimes, however, sermons plod along without much urgency to keep listening.

16. Quoted in Eugene L. Lowry, *The Homiletical Beat: Why All Sermons Are Narrative* (Nashville: Abingdon Press, 2012), 3. Additionally, Lowry quotes Davis: "A sermon is not static like a painting. A painting shows itself as a whole in a single instant. Not only its entire composition, all its subjects and their arrangement, but all its minutest details stand there together, fixed in their intended relation to one another and to the whole. It is a visible design, complete and static. The eye takes it all in at once. A sermon is never like that, never has the objective completeness of a picture or a building" (1).

17. Lowry, *Homiletical Beat*, 3.

Often they do not build from one segment to the next or even within the segment. Other times sermons progress in a scattered fashion, losing the hearers in a bygone era or around a corner or to their mental to-do lists as the preacher turns too sharply onto another path.[18]

One way to help pace your sermon is to insert a cinematic heading whenever and wherever there is a scene change; that is, every time there is a change in physical setting or time frame.[19] This takes minimal time and has the potential for big impact.

```
EXT. SEA OF GALILEE - DAY - 30 CE

[This move/scene/segment highlights the dis-
ciples' strengthened relationship with Jesus.]

INT. FIRST LUTHERAN FELLOWSHIP HALL - DAY -
2019

[This move highlights a recent congregation-
al gathering organized for the purpose of
strengthening their relationship with Jesus.]
```

Inserting such scene headings in our sermon scripts (not as something that would be spoken aloud, but as an organizational tool) is one helpful step in the sermon-revision process. The addition helps us to see if scenes are changing too often or not enough and if they are in the right order. Flashbacks, flash-forwards, and montages, for example, can be very effective as long as they are meaningfully situated. While preachers do not have to worry about the budget with every scene change as the filmmaker does, they would do well to worry about the cost of losing their hearers. We will offer more tips related to sequencing in the next chapter, which focuses on the important work of editing.

Character Development

Presenting biblical characters in effective sermons is more than simply stating their features or actions; it takes some finessing to build the arc, growth, and movement of the character. Just as blue skying in the

18. See section on carding and sermon mapping in chap. 7.

19. McKenzie, *Making a Scene*, 2. McKenzie defines a scene as "the action that takes place in one physical setting in more or less continuous time."

filmmaking writer's room would pose the following questions about characters, so, too, might blue skying in a Bible study. Let's use our John 18 scene as an example.

—Who are the characters and in what way are they integral to the narrative? In John 18, Jesus, Pilate, and the crowd seem to be integral to the narrative, while perhaps the guards are less so. In other words, one need not spend time and energy describing the guards' characteristics and movements. The question then becomes, "Will they play any role in the scene?"

—What are the characters' "wants"? Jesus wants people to understand who he is and is unwavering in his commitment to be that person, even when his life is threatened. Pilate, on the other hand, wants the affirmation of the masses and is willing to frame a blameless being for his own popularity. The increasingly incendiary crowd wants Jesus to be punished and is willing to have a known criminal released from custody for it.

—Where are the characters positioned in the scene (blocked) and to where do they move? How do they move? What motivates them to move? Pilate seems to be moving the most in this scene, which emits a kind of frenetic energy that matches his dialogue. Even the crowd, despite its building energy, stays in place. Jesus, on the other hand, seems quite grounded. This lack of extensive blocking suggests he is on steady ground as one who is confident of who he is.

Other questions one might ask include these:

—How does one character react to another?
—What has happened to this character by the end of the sermon?
—Are there poorly defined characters that are not meshing with one another?
—Are there unlikable characters? If so, do they play an integral role; that is, will the hearers care about them?

In his *Beat Sheet Workbook,* Jamie Nash recommends assembling the cast of characters by filling out a form like this one:[20]

---

20. Jamie Nash, *Save the Cat! Beat Sheet Workbook: How Writers Turn Ideas into Stories* (Los Angeles: Save the Cat! Press, 2022), 122.

Character 1

Name:

Age:

Relationship to hero (circle one):
Family, Friend, Lover, Enemy, Ally, Stranger

Brief physical description:

Dream casting (what actor would best play the character in the movie):

Check the box for how the character relates to their "want":

☐ Rejects the want
☐ Takes the want too far
☐ Teaches the want
☐ Embodies the want
☐ Needs the want
☐ Supports the want

FAITHFUL IMAGINATION

In presermon work, all details are fair game, as long as they are faithful to the biblical account. It takes time to transform characters from ink on the page to multidimensional beings. Eventually, though, the preacher will want to pare down the details to only those that are essential to moving the story along. There is a danger in using too many unnecessary details. We don't need to know that the buttons of her shirt are red unless they will ultimately be of some significance. Everything must mean something. Nothing should be irrelevant. Again, think in terms of filmmaking; every object the crew needs costs money. If it's not significant, it's not worth somebody's time or a portion of the budget.

Remember that preachers write for the ear and not for the eye. It takes time for sound to go from the preacher's mouth to the hearer's ears. Since we're hearing the scene and not seeing it, we need more time to visualize it. So, take your time, but keep the action moving as you conjure the scene for us, from its beginning, through the middle, and all the way to the end. Describe only what our imaginations need to visualize the scene.

A common move in a sermon is to retell the biblical story with some added embellishment. It's as if the reading of the story itself were not enough, as if we assume people are not listening. Of course, eventually, hearers do stop listening because they have become accustomed to the story being retold. Here's a basic retelling:

> In the story you just heard, Pilate enters his headquarters, where Jesus has been held by some guards. Pilate summons Jesus and they have a dialogue in which Pilate questions Jesus's identity. Jesus remains committed to the truth while Pilate is increasingly disturbed by the crowd, who insist that Pilate release another prisoner instead of Jesus.

While these sentences begin to describe the scene and add some details that might be informative and entertaining, the description just plods along, leaving the hearer wondering why it all matters. The "so what?" is not obvious. There is no angle. There is no buildup of energy. There will likely be no impact.

Consider the following example of a sermon move from a preacher who is thinking like a filmmaker when presenting a scene:

> Pilate wastes no breath with niceties once the guards bring Jesus to him. "Are you the king of the Jews?" he asks quickly and forcefully, his widen eyes more than half expecting to receive a straight answer. Instead, the proverbial interview table is turned. "Why? Who's asking?" Jesus dares to ask despite being flanked by two guards at the beck and call of his interrogator.
>
> What follows is a Socratic give-and-take until Pilate stops pacing right in front of Jesus. "So you are a king?"
>
> No doubt Pilate expects a simple yes or no. Instead he gets a calm and steady reply: "For this I was born: To testify to the truth. Everyone who belongs to the truth listens to me."
>
> After receiving silence to his question, "What is truth?" Pilate harrumphs back to the crowd to question them—but not before announcing his verdict. Did you notice it? "I find no case against Jesus." He even refers to him as "the king." But the crowd's insistent jeers deafen any potential for truth; their unison chant is clear. "No. Keep him locked up. Release Barabbas."
>
> The crowd wants control.
>
> Pilate wants public support.
>
> Jesus wants to be known.

The second iteration has the potential to bring the hearers into the world as it reveals the arc of the characters and has a beginning, a middle, and an end. Even more, it sets up the next move in the sermon to be about Jesus's identity not just for those gathered in first-century Jerusalem but also for listeners in the twenty-first century in your city. Mundanely, a sermon move explains key points to be received and remembered. Magically, it can invite hearers into a new world to help them imagine how their own world might be transformed and what their role is in it.

5

Cut by Cut: Editing for Story and Audience

"The film really moved along." "They should've cut it down. It dragged." "It jumped all over the place—I lost the plot." Everyone comments on films, often unaware that they're commenting on the final shaping of the film—the editing. This chapter seeks to make convergences between this final creative stage of filmmaking and the final draft of the sermon. It is time to *"kill your darlings"*—to detach from pet scenes and shots and discard what does not work or belong, no matter how much you're attached to it. This expertise is what the editor brings to the party: a detached, observant eye that is fixed unblinkingly on the audience's experience. For it is the edited version of the story—not the script, the storyboard, or the dailies—that the audience will see. The proverbial buck stops in the editing room. In partnership with the director and producer, the editor creates the final version of the show that will be exhibited to the audience. We will describe the work that happens in the cutting room from the time the editor receives the footage and creates a *rough cut* through screenings and reediting to arrive at the final *locked cut*.

EDITING FILMS

The Role of Editing

> There is the movie that is written, the movie that is shot, and the movie
> that is edited.
> —Film industry adage

The editor relies on the script but views, listens to, and engages most
with the shot footage and sound to cut the show. Directors and editors
alike see the script as a blueprint and the footage as the raw material
to be used and discarded as needed to sculpt the show's final edit. As
director Ang Lee puts it, "Shooting is like buying groceries and the real
cooking is at the editing table."[1]

Editing is more than eliminating bad or boring shots and frames and
selecting the best shots and frames. Good editing is good storytelling.
Many consider the editor to be the show's final rewriter. The editor
sets the show's final order—its sequencing of scenes—not according
to shoot order or script order but according to what makes sense to
tell the story. Movies with heavy-duty visual effects (VFX) along with
those with tons of footage may engage in *postvisualization*, revisiting
storyboards along with dailies during postproduction. Editor-author
Walter Murch (*Apocalypse Now*, *The English Patient*) astutely describes
editing as being "not so much a putting together as it is the discovery
of a path."[2] While it's a path that authors take as well, editors write
with images (shot footage, archival footage, VFX, and graphics such as
titles, captions, and subtitles) and sound (dialogue, *SFX*, and music).
No matter how experienced the editor is, cutting is a trial-and-error
process like writing that requires intuition, reason, and understanding
(that is, living and breathing with the characters).

The Editor's Workflow

The editor receives dailies (the footage shot that day) and then, based
on notes and conversations with the director and notes from the script
supervisor, puts the show together on a computer—a digital editing

1. Quoted in John Lahr, "Becoming the Hulk," *New Yorker*, June 30, 2003.
2. Bernard Weintraub, "Hollywood's Kindest Cuts: Invisible Film Editors
Start to Emerge from Director's Shadow," *New York Times*, August 20, 1998.

system—cut by cut and scene by scene. Over the course of a show there is a lot of footage to view and consider: many different takes and camera angles from production, archival footage, VFX, graphics, sound, and music. It all must be ingested in the digital editing system and organized. The shooting ratio, meaning the ratio of footage shot to footage in the final cut, can range from 4:1 up to 500:1 on a high-budget action feature, the average being 10:1 to 50:1. Murch estimated that in cutting *Apocalypse Now* there were "ninety-five 'unseen' minutes for every minute" in the final product. "For every splice in the finished film there were probably fifteen 'shadow' splices—splices made, considered, and then undone or lifted from the film."[3] Even allowing for those fifteen "shadow splices," Murch writes,

the remaining eleven hours and fifty-eight minutes of each working day were spent in activities that, in their various ways, served to clear and illuminate the path ahead of us: screenings, discussions, rewinding, re-screenings, meetings, scheduling, filing trims, note-taking, bookkeeping, and lots of plain deliberative thought. A vast amount of preparation, really, to arrive at the innocuously brief moment of decisive action: the cut—the moment of transition from one shot to the next—something that, appropriately enough, should look almost self-evidently simple and effortless, if it is even noticed at all.[4]

After reviewing a scene's dailies and absorbing the scene's purpose, with the script (and maybe a strong latte) at hand, the editor will begin to cut. How do editors choose what shot to cut to next? For each cut they will select the superior shot, judging it on several criteria:

1. Action for telling the story
2. Delivery—the take that is best acted, experienced, felt, expressed. Editors stand up for each character in a fiction film or "talking head" in a documentary by putting them in the truest light.
3. Pace—timing most conducive to the flow of the story
4. Technical quality—more critical components are camera, lighting, sound, composition, continuity. Less critical: hair, makeup, wardrobe.

3. Walter Murch, *In the Blink of an Eye: A Perspective on Film Editing*, 2nd ed. (Los Angeles: Silman-James Press, 2001), 4.
4. Murch, *Blink of an Eye*, 4.

Editing Terms

cut. A series of edits. "Cut" and "edit" are used interchangeably: An edit can be made up of cuts, a cut can be made up of edits. The terms are used as both nouns and verbs and understandable in context.

cut point. Also called edit point. Place in a shot where editor decides to cut to another shot. Editors were called "cutters" originally because they physically scissored the film to make edits. The term "cutting room" for the editor's workroom remains today.

edit. Also called cut. The joining together of two different shots or two parts of the same shot to put a show together.

shot. Camera start to camera stop.

take. A shot that starts (or ends) with a camera slate (clapstick) that labels the scene and take. The label might be 13-1, 26A-2, for example.

While there is a plethora of choices for cuts and ways to put a show together, when editors cut for the right reasons and in the right place, they sustain the audience's interest, involvement, and investment in the show. Let's take, for example, a dialogue scene, which typically compose 40 percent or more of a show. To cut a dialogue scene, the editor will concentrate on the relationship between the characters: their looks and reactions as well as their words. As in every scene, the editor will also focus on *continuity*, that is, maintaining physical relationships, actors' performances, camera action, and sound levels from cut to cut. To maintain continuity, an editor makes a *match cut* between elements of actions, wardrobe, props, weather, sound, background, and more. Say the editor is cutting a café scene with two people at a table. The editor will maintain continuity in a number of ways, such as match-cutting characters' eyelines (where they are looking), their performance, their props (e.g., whether their reading glasses are on or off), and the movements of secondary and background characters (servers, other customers, etc.). Editor Carol Littleton (*Body Heat, ET, Places in the Heart*) remarked, "One-to-one dialogue scenes are difficult [to edit] because it's literally about the very thin connection between two people and that connection can't be violated. . . . They may be connecting or not connecting emotionally, but you have to be aware of what's happening between them the whole time."[5]

5. Quoted in Gael Chandler, *Cut by Cut: Editing Your Film or Video*, 2nd ed. (Studio City, CA: Michael Wiese Productions, 2012), 185.

When an editor maintains continuity, the cuts appear seamless to the audience. Akin to listening to an orchestra and hearing the whole symphony and not the individual instruments, moviegoers absorb the film's drama and story and do not notice its cuts. This *invisible editing*, while the norm, is not the rule (serving the story is the only rule), and is regularly countered with discontinuity cuts such as *jump cuts, smash cuts, flash cuts*, obvious *mismatches*, and other obvious, in-your-face cuts that shock or startle.[6] A supreme example of shock cuts is seen in Hitchcock's indelible shower scene in *Psycho* (1960) in which a woman is stabbed to death. At no time does the killer's knife actually touch her body. The editing is rapid—seventy-eight edits in forty-five seconds (the average is twenty to twenty-five per minute)—with varied camera angles: close-ups of her hand, face, and other body parts, the showerhead, shower curtain hooks, a knife, and a shadowy killer. Accompanied by the banal sounds of flowing water, and shrieking music stingers, the scene still frightens today.

Types of Cuts

Editors make many kinds of cuts. To aid our discussion, we've put them in a table and arranged (edited!) them in order of best comprehension.

Type of Cut	Purpose
Cut. The joining together of two different camera shots	To build story and/or show character, idea, or emotion
Reverse. A cut to the opposite (reverse) angle	To show how characters act, react, and interact
POV. A reverse cut that corresponds to where a character is looking	To show what a character is seeing and the audience wants to see too
Cutaway, a.k.a. insert. A cut to a small, significant detail in a scene	To convey necessary information to the audience. Cutaways often act as introductions to scenes or segues between scenes, forwarding the flow of information (usually scene location or time) and the action

continued on next page

6. A 2011 study by Magliano and Zacks used an MRI to examine how different parts of the brain react to classical continuity edits vs. discontinuity edits, and a 2017 study by Heimann et al. used an EEG. See bibliography for a complete reference to these studies.

Type of Cut (cont.)	Purpose (cont.)
Match cut. Duplicating (matching) elements from one shot to another. The elements editors match include screen direction, eyeline, camera angle and framing, props, sound, weather, wardrobe, hair, makeup, lighting, color, and action.	To maintain continuity and narrative flow. The effect is seamless "invisible" edits that the audience doesn't notice since it's engrossed in the story and its characters.
Jump cut. An edit where objects or characters appear to jump because the shot angles are too similar.	To counter continuity and shaft seamless editing to make dramatic points; shorten time; express a character's thoughts, perceptions, dreams, or nightmares; and add or subtract a person or object from a shot.
Dissolve. A transitional cut in which the first/outgoing shot disappears as the second/incoming shot appears.	To portray the passage of time or a change in location or eliminate a jump cut.
Fade-in. A dissolve *to* a filmed shot *from* black or another color.	To slowly begin a show.
Fade-out. A dissolve *from* a filmed shot *to* black or another color.	To slow the pace and give the audience breathing space after a stressful scene, such as a death scene.
Flash cut. A short cut of a few frames that is quick and intense.	To put the audience inside a character's mind with what a character is seeing and feeling.
Smash cut. A short, unexpected cut akin to a surprise slap in the face.	To deliberately jar the audience by zapping the action from one place, object, person, or image to another.

Motivating Cuts

For each cut, the editor asks, "What does the audience need to see, know, or learn next?" No shot goes in simply because of its beauty, crew effort, or cost. Each cut must be motivated to drive the action, the flow, and the thought process forward, knitting the story together for viewers, cut by cut.

Editing, as it seeks to plant the show inside the audience's head, is the part of filmmaking that is closest to human thought, emotion, and experience. To accomplish this, editors juxtapose all types of camera angles including *master shots* and *reverses,* close-ups and other *cutaways.* However, editing is not a strictly cerebral endeavor. Editors use their heart and instinct as much as their mind to read the footage. They cut from the gut. Reflecting on *Battleship Potemkin* (1925), director-editor Sergei Eisenstein said, "The filmed material at the moment of editing can sometimes be wiser than the author or editor. I realized the emotive scenes as the Holy Scriptures say, 'without seeing my creation'; that is, I realized them thanks to the feelings which the events inspired within me."[7]

Pacing Cuts

> How you intercut is so important because there's rhythm, there's pace, there's emotional drama taking place. If you're on something too long, then you lose power in the next scene. There's rhythms within a scene, and there's rhythms that are going to move the scene forward.
> —Editor Michael Kahn, *Raiders of the Lost Ark, Schindler's List, Jurassic Park, West Side Story*[8]

Some scenes go tick . . . tick . . . tick . . . Others, tick, tick, tick. Still others, tickticktick. Why? Because editing changes the timing and duration of the filmed shots to long, medium, and short cuts, creating a new pace for the audience. Akin to musical compositions, edited scenes and sequences contain a myriad of rhythms as well as climaxes, denouements, pauses, rests, and interludes. It's not hard to picture the different pacing of a frenetic battle scene, as in *All Quiet on the Western Front* (2022); a common dialogue scene, such as those between Rick and Ilsa in *Casablanca* (1942); or the slow-paced opening of many a Western as the characters ride into town, as in *Once upon a Time in the West* (1969). Time-altering cuts are routine in film editing as time is compressed or expanded: an embrace is elongated via cuts of different angles, a ten-month journey shrinks to a ten-second montage, or a life is portrayed in a ninety-minute biopic. The cinematically literate audience absorbs them all.

7. From the writings of film theorist and director Sergei Eisenstein, as quoted by Ralph Rosenblum and Robert Karen in *When the Shooting Stops . . . the Cutting Begins: A Film Editor's Story* (New York: Viking Press, 1979), 57.
    8. Weintraub, "Hollywood's Kindest Cuts."

Certain VFX also play with time to evoke places, eras, or ideas and can portray a character's perspective. Here are a few examples. Filmmakers frequently use slo mo to break down the action, increase the tension, and show how characters react to a situation. A slo mo hail of bullets intercut with regular motion and jump cuts took out the titular couple in *Bonnie and Clyde* (1967) in a shocking yet balletic scene. *Speedups* move things along and are often comic, but they can also show POV. In *The Diving Bell and the Butterfly* (2007), the shots speed up as the main character recovers his memory. A *freeze-frame* stops time and is often created to defy death and immortalize characters, as the freeze-frames that end *Butch Cassidy and the Sundance Kid* (1969) and *Thelma and Louise* (1991) do. When a filmmaker uses *reverse motion* (plays a shot backward), time appears to go backward. Reverse motion can create a comical or magical effect or demonstrate how something was done, such as how a murder was carried out, in *Hot Fuzz* (2007). In *Slumdog Millionaire* (2008), reverse motion shows the hero reliving his past as he races through a train station to reunite with his beloved and the Oscar-winning movie reaches its climax.

Editing is a rhythmic dance of images, sounds, and music, all created by the duration, placement, and pacing of the cuts. If you think the dance has sped up over time, you are correct. In 1929, cuts had an average shot length (*ASL*) of 11.2 seconds; the ASL today is 2.5 seconds. Not only editing has sped up, of course. We think nothing of watching TV and darting to the crawl of news at the bottom of the screen while checking or sending a message on a phone or iPad. Shorter ASLs are part of the *MTV effect* and have been studied by Cornell cognitive psychology professor James Cutting and his graduate students.[9] They measured the duration of every shot in every scene from 150 popular Hollywood movies filmed between 1935 and 2005 in five genres: action, adventure, animation, comedy, and drama. Applying a concept from chaos theory that describes a pattern of attention occurring naturally in the human brain, the researchers found that films made after 1980 matched the natural rhythm of the mind. They deduced that this pattern developed during the lifespan of filmmaking as the edited

---

9. "MTV effect" is a loose term for a type of filmmaking born with MTV that uses handheld camera movements and multiple cuts, VFX, and story lines while drastically decreasing dialogue and letting music dominate the (sometimes thin) story.

rhythms of shot sequences created or failed to create clear and engaging movies, and observed, "Modern movies may be more engrossing—we get 'lost' in them more readily—because the universe's natural rhythm is driving the mind."[10]

In additional studies, Cutting and his students researched the reasons for the diminishing ASLs, noting that current feature films contain more motion, *parallel action*, and close-ups than earlier films. Modern movies also eschew dissolves for cuts, show fewer characters on-screen at the same time, and have shorter scenes and sequences. All these factors make it easier for viewers to take in movies and TV shows more swiftly. Our conclusion is that whether the pace of the cutting is fast, medium, or slow, it must gain the trust and engagement of the audience to have impact.

Scene Transitions

As an editor works through a show, completing scene after scene (in the nonlinear order that they're normally shot in), they decide how best to transition from one scene to another. They will use a cut, a *dissolve,* a *wipe,* or some other type of VFX, depending on the pacing of both the outgoing and incoming scene. Audio plays a significant role: dialogue often overlaps cuts and scenes; music smooths transitions between scenes and sequences and within a montage; and sound effects do the same, especially background sounds such as wind or waves. Transitions between scenes can be quick, to keep the pace going, or slow, as with a long dissolve, when the audience needs a pause to detach from the impact of the outgoing scene and ease into the incoming scene.

From Rough Cut to Locked Cut

The first pass an editor makes, called the rough cut, is the first complete telling of the story with picture and sound. The editor screens this first cut with the director. With all the planning and prepping— the many sets of eyes on the script, the storyboarding, the director shooting supported by a host of crew members—you might think

---

10. James Cutting, Jordan DeLong, and Christine Nothelfer, "Attention and the Evolution of Hollywood Film," *Psychological Science Online*, February 5, 2010.

that the footage would swiftly and easily come together in the editing room. It may, but there are always problems demanding lesser and greater attention. Following the rough cut, there's much more grappling with the story to be done. The editor and the director view the entire show, then screen it scene by scene to discuss problems and solutions. The editor makes notes of all the changes to be made and recuts the film. This process—screening, making change notes, recutting— repeats for days, weeks, or months and involves major changes as well as fine-tuning.

Reediting

> The practice of reinventing is an ever-evolving, never-ending process. Every day, every moment, we must be willing to let go of what came before. . . . We must eat of "fresh manna." That's why the Lord's Prayer says, "Give us this day our daily bread." It doesn't say, "Give us this week our daily bread," or "Give us enough bread to last through pilot season!"
> —Derek Rydall, *There's No Business like Soul Business*

To continue with Ang Lee's cooking metaphor from above, the first cut makes evident what is cooking and coming together and what isn't. To diagnose the problems, the editor and the director (on feature films) or executive producer (in TV) will scrutinize the story, the characters, and the performances. They will run scenes, sequences, and the show over and over and over again and make many versions as they work toward the final, locked cut. With each cut, they will decide which scenes are vital and revisit their structure and order, eyes fixed on the audience and what "plays."

Filmmakers resolve story problems by deleting, rearranging, intercutting, truncating, or expanding scenes. Exposition, backstory, climax, the ending—all plot holes are pored over and fixed or massaged. Scenes can be reordered or reshot and new scenes picked up if necessary and financially feasible. At times a scene or an entire show is reedited from scratch. Every frame of the show is examined and then *trimmed* or extended as needed to make sure it delivers the proper flow of information to and experience for the audience. If the action goes by too quickly for viewers to grasp, the pacing is loosened up. If the pace drags, the editors tighten up dialogue, reactions, and actions. Like the stone causing the proverbial ripple in the pond, every change, even if only a frame or two, affects subsequent cuts as the rhythm has been recalibrated. Deleted scenes may be put back in. Famously, Dorothy singing "Somewhere over the Rainbow" at the beginning of *The Wizard of Oz* was on the chopping block because the studio head and producer found it degrading for her to sing in a barnyard and believed that children—the movie's intended audience—would tune out. The director and two producers fought to keep the now immortal scene.

During reediting, filmmakers experiment and see what sings and what falls flat. Words, dialogue, images, and scenes may be repeated or overlapped to depict multiple points of view or angles of an event. *Groundhog Day* (1993), *Hero* (2002), and *The Eternal Sunshine of the Spotless Mind* (2004) repeat scenes and images as the characters relive experiences. Repeated phrases can be iconic: "Here's looking at you, kid," from *Casablanca* (1942); "May the force be with you" from *Star Wars* or comic such as Sandy Dennis's "Oh my god!" refrain in *The Out-of-Towners* (1970) and Jack Black's cell phone message in *The Big Year* (2011) periodically chirping, "Bird, bird, bird; bird is the word." This *anaphora*—repeating of words, phrases, or sentences—strengthens ideas and creates rhythm and unity, searing words, images, or scenes into the viewer's brain, as does Gertrude Stein's "A rose is a rose is a rose" poem and the Rev. Martin Luther King's "I Have a Dream" speech.

Filmmakers also fine-tune characters and performances during reediting to make sure that every gesture, word, look, and action counts. They polish documentary interviews so that interviewees are understandable and true to themselves. Some characters and interviews are stripped down or, occasionally, left on the cutting room floor (deleted on the digital editing system)—all in service of the narrative. Filmmakers pay attention to sound and music, adding and improving tracks. They may add narration to see if it will help the story, or they may change narrators. Director Sarah Polley changed the narrator of *Women Talking* (2022) from a male adult to a teenage girl during postproduction because the girl fit the story better.[11]

---

11. Devan Coggan, "Director Sarah Polley Explains How 'Many Voices' Made *Women Talking*," *Entertainment Weekly*, December 24, 2022, https://ew.com /movies/women-talking-sarah-polley-interview/.

Prescreenings

After a number of recuts it's time for test screening the show. Film-makers invite their friends and peers to give them feedback or test-screen the picture with as much finished VFX, sound effects, and music as possible for a theater audience. They may select a small focus group from the larger audience to provide feedback on areas of concern.

Following the test screenings, editors return to the cutting room for more recuts. At last, they will make the final edit and lock the show.

EDITING SERMONS

As effortless as it might seem, "a film is a universe where chance is never an excuse for anything. . . . It is a series of hundreds of very particular decisions, and every single one of them must be felt. That is the agony and the satisfaction of the process."[12] The same is true in preaching. (Yes, sometimes the "agony" bit as well.) While some might insert "Holy Spirit" for the word "chance," even then, it is often said that crafting sermons is 10 percent inspiration and 90 percent perspiration. Part of the 90 percent is coming up with content, but another part is the arrangement of that content. That's where editing comes in.

The wisdom of film editors can help preachers avoid three common missteps that keep sermons from having the most impact. The first is including too many elements that do not advance the narrative movement of the sermon. The second occurs when the progression of these elements does not make sense. No doubt the culprit could be a lack of time to revise a sermon "rough cut," which is a third misstep. Sondra Willobee asserts, "When we leave our preparation to the last minute, we deprive ourselves of one of the most effective sermon techniques available: revision."[13]

So, preachers, if you avoid beginning to craft a sermon too late, leaving little time to edit, you can begin to address the challenge of not knowing what to change once you have the rough cut. Enter: the

12. Jon Boorstin, *Making Movies Work: Thinking like a Filmmaker* (Los Angeles: Silman-James Press, 1995), 6.

13. Sondra Willobee, *The Write Stuff: Crafting Sermons That Capture and Convince* (Louisville, KY: Westminster John Knox Press, 2009), 103.

wisdom of film editors. The remainder of this chapter will explore five key takeaways from film editing that give preachers concrete ways to revise a sermon for maximum impact:

1. Remember that the process is not just cerebral; it is also emotional.
2. Remove everything that does not advance the narrative.
3. Recognize that sequencing is an act of pastoral care.
4. Use the variety of cuts (film) / transitions (sermons) available.
5. Host a test screening.

A Cerebral and Emotional Process

Preachers do not judge their success on a parishioner greeting them at the end of worship with a handshake and "Wow, preacher, you are so adept at your transitions" or "You had the perfect amount of sermon moves offered in just the right order. Thank you." But being adept at transitions and knowing what and where to revise is likely to lead to a satisfying "Your sermon made me feel like I belong" or "Thank you for the confidence-building sermon. I think I'm ready to speak out more against the injustices I see happening in our community." As with film editing, the goal of sermon editing is not to call attention to the editing itself but to help the congregation get swept up in hearing the sermon and lose the awareness that they are listening to a sermon.

Just as film editors put themselves in the shoes of the audience, effective preachers imagine how their sermons will be received from the pew as they craft the sermon. They ask cerebral questions: Will this make sense? Is the flow of ideas logical? Have I offered enough background information? Is my language too academic or, perhaps, too simple for these people? However, to ask only the intellectual questions is to cheat the hearers. In addition, preachers must ask: How will the sermon impact the congregation emotionally? Into what experience of the human condition and of God does it invite them? Will it offend? Will they be ready to hear this?

For Walter Murch, emotion tops the list of what makes an effective cut. Cut from the gut. "*How do you want the audience to feel?* If they are feeling what you want them to feel all the way through the film, you've done about as much as you can ever do. What they finally remember is not the editing, not the camerawork, not the performances, not even the story—it's how they felt."[14] How much more true this is for the preacher for whom the task of revising sermons requires heart and instinct as much as mind when "reading the footage." Preaching is both an art and a science; it takes both perspiration and inspiration.

Removing Everything Not Advancing the Narrative

Be Discerning about "Shot" Choices

A preacher's raw footage typically comes from their deep exegetical engagement with Scripture, observing their community's needs, reading the words of biblical and theological scholars, and even sensing what the Holy Spirit might be nudging them to say. Most often there is more material available to a preacher than can fit into a sermon. Preachers must be discerning about which "shot" best represents what they want the audience to see, hear, and experience. The equivalent of shots for the preacher includes moves such as telling a personal story, imaginatively exploring what an experience might have been like for the character in the story, connecting the biblical story to a congregation's mission statement, teaching on church doctrine, offering encouraging words to a community in crisis, or exhorting people to care for their neighbors in ways that align with Jesus's radical compassion and hospitality. For each of these moves, there are likely numerous possible "takes."

Recall Walter Murch's comments about those "ninety-five 'unseen' minutes for every minute" in the final version of *Apocalypse Now*. Student preachers often say after a thorough exegetical process, "Now, what do I do with all of this information? I'm more confused than ever." In the same way that a majority of the editor's time is not spent splicing film, the majority of the preacher's time is not spent typing on the computer, but thinking.

The encouraging thing is that there is not necessarily one right way. There might be some wrong ways, but there are many right ways. Given all the same material, no two preachers will structure a sermon

14. Murch, *Blink of an Eye*, 19.

in precisely the same way. Ask these questions: What's the wrong way, and what is most suitable for the occasion?

What preachers say from the pulpit should not be a willy-nilly, throw-a-bunch-of-stuff-out-there-and-see-what-sticks kind of operation. Consider what might stick, yes, but do so before you step into the pulpit. Be prepared to set aside what might not stick, including, and perhaps especially, your favorite sections, be they insights, illustrations, connections, stories, jokes, or exhortations.

"Kill Your Darlings"

Pardon the violent imagery, but "kill your darlings" is a phrase used to exhort creatives to get rid of their pet (some say self-indulgent) scenes to serve the greater good of the work. In the same way that filmmakers know that moviegoers will not sit for a four-hour film (nor will their budgets allow for it), preachers know the time expectations of their parishioners. If the sermon lasts longer than that range, the congregation will become impatient and stop listening.

Screenwriter Dustin Lance Black (*Milk, Rustin*) expresses how difficult it is to cut out one's own creative work: "It's painful because you've done so much work to gather all of these interviews and this information and 90 percent is gone. Ninety percent of it you'll never use. These are the land of lost scenes. These are my precious children I've had to kill. . . . How can I not have this scene? How can I not have that?"[15]

Murch speaks of "killing one's darlings" in the cutting process just as violently: "We chop up the poor film in a miniature guillotine and then stick the dismembered pieces together like Dr. Frankenstein's monster. The difference (the miraculous difference) is that out of this apparent butchery our creation can sometimes gain not only a life but a soul as well."[16]

Is that not what we preachers are hoping for as well? We hope to breathe life into these words as if they were dry bones ready to live—as if we are dry bones awaiting new life. It might be true that a certain story or a particular theological point has, in and of itself, the capacity to enliven the hearers. But as in a film, no scene or beat or shot is an island unto

15. Scott W. Smith, "How an Oscar-Winning Screenwriter Uses Index Cards," *Screenwriting from Iowa* (blog), May 2, 2017, https://screenwritingfromiowa.word
-press.com/2017/05/02/how-an-oscar-winning-screenwriter-uses-index-cards/.

16. Murch, *Blink of an Eye*, 57.

itself. (Again, no shot goes in simply because of its beauty, crew effort, or cost.) The sinews and flesh must connect bone to bone. It's not enough to have five to seven great ideas. They need to fit together. For each successive cut, the preacher, like the film editor, asks, "What do I want to see, know, learn, or reveal next?" Even more, "What do I want the audience to see and hear and experience?" When choosing and sequencing "takes," preachers are encouraged not to just put them together in the most orderly way but to ask, "How can people best hear the material in this sermon?" because "sermon structure is about shaping communication, not merely about organizing information. A sermon form is a plan for the experience of listening, not just an arrangement of data."[17]

The preacher goes about "trimming everything that doesn't advance the theme" by remembering that "purpose drives form."[18] Here we return to the importance of impact. In preaching, this is called the sermon's function, and it requires that the preacher make sure that each sermon move advances the hoped-for impact and cut everything that does not. While that opening joke might get a laugh, if it does not set up what is coming later in the sermon in a serious way or guide people to a deeper relationship with Jesus, cut it.

Take, for example, exposition or background story. For both of these story elements, less is more. The film editor discovers it may not be necessary to show a montage that begins with the moment of the protagonist's birth, followed by an establishing shot of their current home before getting to the conflict—an argument with their kids in the living room. By focusing on the body language during the living room dialogue scene, perhaps with an occasional close-up of family photographs on the mantel, the editor informs the audience about the protagonist's current conflict as well as their backstory. The same is true in preaching: the preacher need not reiterate the entire story that was read just a few minutes earlier. After offering an "establishing shot" followed by a transitional phrase, zoom in to the action of the scene of the living room. Let the hearers fill in the surroundings after you've given them what they need to do so. Here's an example of what editing the sermon's rough cut might look like.

17. Thomas G. Long, *The Witness of Preaching*, 3rd ed. (Louisville, KY: Westminster John Knox Press, 2016), 143–44. Long goes on to say, "The shape of a sermon is not merely a convenient and logical way to arrange content; it is an invitation to—perhaps even a demand upon—the hearers to listen to the content according to a particular pattern. As such, form significantly influences what happens to the hearer in and through the sermon."

18. Willobee, *Write Stuff*, 110.

	Rough Cut	**Final Cut**
Film	We see: • a montage of the protagonist's (P's) birth • EXT. Establishing shot of P's home • INT. P's home • Medium wide shot: P argues with spouse as kids distance themselves	We see: • INT. P's home, close-ups of family photos on the mantel as we hear a couple arguing • Medium wide shot: P argues with spouse as kids distance themselves.
Sermon	Let me tell you about Curt, one who is crying out in his own wilderness. Curt was born in a small town in Pennsylvania when the coal industry was taking a hit as a result of the emerging concerns for the environment. His father was a miner, and his mother was the daughter of a miner. His house was the smallest on the block of single-family homes turned into duplexes. The one-bedroom side of the duplex was sparsely furnished but had a new bassinet that only fit in the doorway to his parents' bedroom. The bedroom was so small that the door had to be kept open so that the bassinet could fit in the doorway. Curt is now grown and has inherited that family home. It's still only one side of the duplex, and Curt now finds that his third child's bassinet still doesn't fit in the bedroom without keeping the door open. His older two children share a makeshift bedroom that used to be the northwest corner of the living room. These tight	Let me tell you about one who is crying out in his own wilderness as he struggles to raise a family in a small town south of Scranton, Pennsylvania. Entering Curt's small duplex, we see a lineup of framed photos on the mantel. • There's Curt as a baby in his new bassinet that blocks the doorway to his parents' bedroom. • Another with his mother holding him alongside his father and grandfather on break from the coal mines. • Another frame holds a local newspaper clipping of the whole family on the picket lines to save coal mining jobs from environmentalists. • The biggest frame features a family of five—with three kids ranging in age from five to five months. In the background, we hear Curt and his wife arguing over an unexpected bill. The newborn is

continued on next page

	Rough Cut (cont.)	Final Cut (cont.)
Sermon (cont.)	quarters have always been tough, but the COVID pandemic has exacerbated the tension. Curt and his wife, Sheila, argue almost daily. When they do, the baby cries and the two older kids try to get away from the tension. Cindy is five and hates when her mom and dad fight. The teachers have noticed. Curt Jr. just mimics his big sister. So when she cries, he cries. When she yells, he yells. When she hides, he hides.	crying and the two older kids are hiding in their makeshift bedroom that used to be the northwest corner of the living room. The tension in the tight quarters has increased during COVID, compelling Curt to run out the back door, throw his hands up and scream . . . and scream and scream . . . until he's breathless.

Note how unnecessary details were removed and the words show more than they tell.

The process of collecting all the possibilities to be included in a sermon is quite nonlinear. While we are starting our scriptural exegesis, contemporary sermon imagery is already popping into our minds. While we are typing up a rough draft of a manuscript, a new key exegetical observation can arise that changes our perspective. But discontinuity is not desired in the final product. Sure, preachers' thoughts jump around while they are in their study, first reading the context of the pericope, studying its history, facilitating a Bible study on it with parishioners, imaging a possible powerful closing. But, in the end, during the delivery from the pulpit, continuity reigns. Editing is "the convenient means by which discontinuity is rendered continuous."[19] (See chap. 7, which describes a common process with index cards—carding—that screenwriters use for rewriting and sequencing.)

Sequencing as an Act of Pastoral Care

Taking the time to review the parts of a sermon for the most effective order is vital to its potential for impact and meaning. Essentially this is the wide-shot work of crafting the sermon's form. Sermon form need not be prescriptive or complicated, but it is simply an "organization

19. Murch, *Blink of an Eye*, 9.

plan for deciding what kinds of things will be said and done in a sermon and in what sequence."[20] In Wes Allen's words, "By sermonic form, we mean the overarching rhetorical structure of the sermon—the intentional ordering of ideas and imagery designed to convey a specific gospel message and offer a particular experience of that message to a particular congregation."[21]

Remember the editor's call to stand in the shoes of the audience when making certain cuts. The call is even louder for the preacher who wishes to bear witness to the claim of the gospel on the lives of the congregation. How will that claim be heard and received? Long goes so far to say that "fleshing out a basic sermon form is, in many ways, an act of pastoral care."[22]

Pastoral care includes meeting people where they are, discerning what motivates them and what opens their hearts and ears to hearing what others have to say, as well as including divergent viewpoints. Launching one exhortation after another at people is not gracious and likely is ineffective because most people do not want to be told what to do even if they know something must change. Expanding one's repertoire of sermon forms to offer a variety of ways a listener might hear sermons respects the claim that "no one form is adequate to display the fullness of the gospel."[23]

> A sermon's form, as we have argued, is part of its meaning, and if a congregation is treated week after week only to the problem-solving design, it is inevitably being subtly taught that the purpose of the gospel is to resolve problems or that the best experience of hearing the gospel is a deeply felt "Aha!" Sometimes the gospel does not resolve ambiguity; it creates it. Sometimes the gospel does not come to us as an Aha!—an unexpected word surprising us or turning our world upside down—but instead as a familiar and trusted word of confirmation, as the "old, old story."[24]

Allen, too, argues that "different forms offer hearers different experiences of the gospel—different ways of thinking, of feeling, and of acting. . . . Different forms do this differently. This form primarily engages

20. Long, *Witness of Preaching*, 136.

21. O. Wesley Allen, Jr., *Determining the Form* (Minneapolis: Fortress Press, 2018), 2.

22. Long, *Witness of Preaching*, 72.

23. Long, *Witness of Preaching*, 56.

24. Long, *Witness of Preaching*, 150.

the hearer's mind, that one the hearer's heart, and another that person's hands. If we want our preaching to help our hearers love God with their whole heart, soul, strength, and mind, then we must utilize different forms that over time engage the whole person of the listener."[25]

Editing sermons can bring the words of Scripture (and people?) to life. Revising a sermon's rough cut is the act of pastoral care that moves beyond simply saying what needs to be said to getting something to be heard.[26] When editing, preachers must also consider pacing, which is yet another act of pastoral care because it helps the hearers hear.

On Pacing

"The middle section dragged." "There was so much happening at the closing that I got lost and then it was over." These time-oriented statements about experiencing a film sound a lot like what someone might say of a sermon: "OK, I got it, move on" or "The preacher seemed to make some good points, but there wasn't time to let it sink in." Remember, preaching is more akin to the temporal arts than the visual arts, which is why preaching and filmmaking are fruitful partners. A sermon is an ordered form of moving time—a kind of temporal sequencing.[27] Consider the time signature of your sermon.

Like a film editor, preachers can tighten and loosen pacing by being intentional about their time-altering cuts. For example, notice the number of times a preacher moves back and forth between past and present—typically between first-century CE and the current century. This leap is not too surprising given that the New Testament provides an account of first-century events of Jesus and his followers. However, this 2,000-year leap leaves people in the pews dizzy and exhausted with a kind of homiletical jet lag. This leap is so common in preaching that congregation members have become used to it. But they shouldn't have to. Even filmmakers know that whether the pace of the cutting is fast, medium, or slow, the goal is to gain the trust and engagement of the audience.

25. Allen, *Determining the Form*, 5.

26. Fred Craddock wisely remarks that getting the gospel to be heard (not just saying it) is the goal for preachers, in *Preaching* (Nashville: Abingdon Press, 1985), 167.

27. Eugene L. Lowry, *The Homiletical Beat: Why All Sermons Are Narrative* (Nashville: Abingdon Press, 2012), 2.

This isn't to say that one cannot move back and forth in time. But any cut that is a "sudden disruption of reality" must be chosen to that end.[28] Whether your sermon's pacing is fast, medium, or slow, give hearers time to catch up by orienting them to each new era and space. If you cannot do that, linger a bit longer in one era before moving to another. It is true that we've become accustomed to a faster pace both in reality and on the screen. We are able to keep up because of the choice of transitional cuts an editor makes to take us from one scene or time period to the next. The same can be true with transitions in sermons. The options are as abundant for the preacher as they are for the film editor.

Effective pacing is not just the rate at which the preacher speaks, and it's not just about duration and number of pauses; it is taking into consideration how much hearers can handle and in what order. Again, think in emotional and cerebral terms. Too much information given too quickly is difficult to receive. If you drop an emotional bomb, your hearers need a moment. If you wallop them with one heavy theological concept after another, they might shut down. If you offer a long list of, for example, ways the world is not acting according to God's will, be mindful of the order of that list. And limit it if you can. Sometimes, less is more. Pacing decisions are about speed, quantity, and sequencing.[29] They are also about transitioning from one section to another.

Diversifying Your Transitions

The art of choosing just the right phrase for the right moment of the sermon is not lost on the preacher. In fact, sometimes we agonize over finding just the right word. Preachers spend time on the particular phrases that serve as transitions from one major move to the other whether that be a temporal or geographical change.

Watch a section of a film until you've identified two or three scene changes. Then take a closer look at the transitions themselves.

—How does the filmmaker guide us from one scene to the next?

28. Murch, *Blink of an Eye*, 16.

29. Preachers are encouraged to "map" their sermons in much the same way some screenwriters "card" their screenplays. See chap. 7 for a description of sermon mapping.

—What hints in the previous scene suggest where we will be moving to a new scene?

—Is the scene transition smooth? abrupt? What makes you say that?

—What effect does the scene change have on the viewer?

Now return to your sermon draft and analyze its transitions using similar questions. The first step is to make sure that you have made transitions. Second, identify the roles the transitions play. Do you always use the same kind of transitions? Are your transitions creative and not cliché? There are common transitions in sermons; for example, "In today's Gospel reading . . ." You've heard it. You've said it. But why not be more creative? When you begin to talk about Peter, hearers will know you are referring to the section of Scripture that was just read. Therefore, you need not say, "In today's Gospel reading" (or an equivalent). Instead, if you are transitioning from a contemporary story to something that happened with Jesus and his disciples, try this transition: "We weren't the first to be in awe of Jesus's capacity to calm the treacherous seas of life. The disciples saw it firsthand."

This continuity is more engaging; we want to move (or be moved) seamlessly from one major section to the next. Thinking in film-editing terms, match cuts or cutaways yield a kind of sermonic invisible editing. Consider the following examples:

Type of Transition	Sermon Example	Notes
Match cut. An edit (cut) for continuity in which the majority of the elements are duplicated (matched) from the first shot to the second shot. Examples: Wardrobe (eyeglasses, clothing, etc.), hairdo, makeup, weather, action (walking, running, turning, etc.)	**Move**: The preacher spends some time reminding the congregation how difficult it was thirty years earlier as they began their ministry in a new neighborhood. **Transition**: "We are that same community. Yes. And yet, in so many ways we are not." **Move**: The preacher affirms how the congregation has grown, spiritually and in numbers, in order to make a positive impact in the community.	The preacher refers to the same congregation, but moves from one time frame to another; in this case, three decades ago to the present. In effect, the preacher is match cutting from the congregation in the past to the congregation in the present.

continued on next page

Type of Transition (cont.)	Sermon Example (cont.)	Notes (cont.)
Cutaway. Any shot—ordinarily a close-up—that is used to cut away from the main action in the master shot. Examples: Close-up of a map where treasure is buried, a person's hands trembling	**Move**: The preacher spends some time reminding the congregation how difficult it was thirty years earlier as they began their ministry in a new neighborhood. **Transition**: The preacher focuses specifically on one person in the congregation who was instrumental in helping them through that difficult time. **Move**: The preacher invites the congregation to name out loud people who have been witnesses, saints, or encouragers for them.	The cutaway allows the preacher to zoom in on individuals of the past before identifying faithful leaders in the present.

While invisible editing seamlessly and satisfyingly moves things along, it need not be the rule. Again, the only rule is that the choice serves the story in film or the overall hoped-for impact on the hearer in preaching. Abrupt cuts can create a desired effect in ways smoothly invisible match cuts cannot. Sometimes discontinuity effectively creates a desired tension. The preacher can use, for example, a kind of flash cut that is mentally jarring. While it's not "*visual* displacement"[30] that preachers are after, there is a kind of auditory displacement or disorientation. Consider the following examples of sermonic transitions as equivalent to a film editor's smash cuts and flash cuts:

---

30. Murch, *Blink of an Eye*, 6.

Type of Transition	Sermon Example	Notes
Smash cut. An unexpected, lightning-quick cut designed to jar the audience by zapping the action from one place, object, person, or image to another. Example: A car comes out of nowhere and crashes into another car.	**Move**: The preacher spends some time reminding the congregation how difficult it was thirty years ago as they began their ministry in a new neighborhood. **Transition**: The preacher makes a brief analogy to the Israelites wandering in the wilderness for forty years. **Move**: The preacher affirms how the congregation has grown, spiritually and in numbers, in order to make a positive impact in the community.	This kind of cut/transition can be effective if the preacher returns to, in this case, a move on the Israelites. If the preacher does not, then the abruptness of the smash cut can be jarring at best and, at worst, can lose the hearer altogether. Films use smash cuts sparingly, and preachers are encouraged to do the same.
Flash cut. A short cut of a few frames that quickly and intensely gets inside a character's mind. Example: A character remembers a past trauma and then quickly refocuses on the present.	**Move**: The preacher spends some time reminding the congregation how difficult it was thirty years ago as they began their ministry in a new neighborhood. **Transition**: "For some of you, important friendships were at stake. For others, you may have considered leaving the congregation. The pain you felt when some dear members left the church altogether is still palpable for some of you." **Move**: "And yet you persevered." The preacher then affirms how the congregation has grown, spiritually and in numbers, in order to make a positive impact in the community.	This transition is like a flash cut in that it momentarily prompts hearers to "flash" to memories of the people described, thereby getting the hearer to get into the emotional space of the past before moving to the present to highlight the congregation's perseverance. The flash cut makes the sentence "And yet you persevered" all the more affirming.

Film editors view cuts over and over, engaging in a kind of trial and error to see how best to flow the story and information to the audience. The equivalent for preachers is to speak their sermons out loud, trying different transitions in order to hear which options require too big of a leap and which might be most fitting. Another way to assess one's choices is to test them on actual hearers, which is where we turn next.

Audience Prescreenings

As the "ombudsman for the audience,"[31] film editors are closest to the viewers because they are typically not privy to the context of the film's creation. Because in most circumstances preachers serve as the sermon's screenwriter, cinematographer, and director and are thereby privy to the context of a sermon's creation, being the editor can be difficult. So instead of just imagining a sermon's effect on people in the pew, practice a more collaborative preaching process, as emphasized earlier in the book, and test the sermon's impact with some listeners by hosting a prescreening. This process might be as comprehensive as preaching the whole sermon and getting input from a group of people or simply checking in briefly with another person about a particular illustration you anticipate will ground an abstract theological concept.

While practicing the sermon aloud is an important benefit of this step, the main benefit is to learn how others hear the sermon draft to determine whether and how impact matches intent. For example, a preacher might think he is affirming all people and their circumstances by saying, "It doesn't matter if you are black or white, rich or poor, male or female, gay or straight, you are welcome here." And yet, when "rehearsing" the delivery of the sermon (or part of a sermon) in front of another, the preacher discovers the impact of the words is hurtful because they suggest that the particularities of one's experience don't matter. Even more, they reinforce simplistic and unhelpful binaries. Upon learning that the impact did not mirror the good intentions, the preacher can adjust accordingly.

Director Fred Zinnemann asserts that what the last 10 percent of the film *Julia* (1977) needed was "the participation of the audience, whom he saw as his 'final collaborators.'"[32] Getting "notes" (written

---

31. Murch, *Blink of an Eye*, 24.

32. Murch, *Blink of an Eye*, 52. Many of the ideas in this section can be found in Murch's chapter "Test Screenings: Referred Pain," 52–56.

or verbal) from actual people need not force the preacher to change everything. Walter Murch recommends that editors wait a few days rather than nix a whole scene that received negative feedback. "The impulse is to 'fix' the scene or cut it out. But the chances are that that scene is fine. Instead, the problem may be that the audience simply didn't understand something that they needed to know for the scene to work." Murch advocates treating some comments like "referred pain." He says one should not operate on the elbow until you're sure the problem isn't a pinched nerve in the shoulder. The audience will "simply tell you where the pain is" and maybe not "the source of the pain."[33]

In the same way, preachers need not "fix" every last concern the hearers express, because they may be simply expressing where the pain is and not identifying the source of pain. A prescreening of sorts is not simply giving people what they want to hear, but testing what is heard so that the proclamation can most effectively announce good news. This kind of testing can be especially helpful when the preacher plans to address a social issue that is divisive, potentially triggering or possibly causing some to say, "politics do not belong in the pulpit."

Ultimately, the way preachers preach guides the audience for how they should listen. Perhaps a prescreening process helps a preacher understand that they have been trying too hard to control how listeners react. Murch says that the "overactive editor who changes shots too frequently" can be compared to "a tour guide who can't stop pointing things out,"[34] and adds,

> If the guide—that is to say, the editor—doesn't have the confidence to let people themselves occasionally choose what they want to look at, or to leave things to their imagination, then he is pursuing a goal (complete control) that in the end is self-defeating. People will eventually feel constrained and then resentful from the constant pressure of his hand on the backs of their necks.[35]

Murch continues, "Some of the time you just want to walk around and see what *you* see." In general, people in the pews want to be trusted to participate. "Because you want to do only what is necessary to engage the imagination of the audience—suggestion is always more effective

33. Murch, *Blink of an Eye*, 55.
34. Murch, *Blink of an Eye*, 16.
35. Murch, *Blink of an Eye*, 16.

than exposition. Past a certain point, the more effort you put into a wealth of detail, the more you encourage the audience to become spectators rather than participants."[36]

If preachers start the sermon-crafting process only a few days before Sunday, they will not get past a rough cut to a locked cut. If preachers begin in advance (and perhaps commit to working on more than one sermon at a time—especially if the lectionary readings follow one another week after week), then perhaps around Thursday morning they can begin to hone the rough cut. It's also true that the more preachers engage the best practices of film editors, the more naturally those practices will become part of the process. Call it invisible editing.

In the preface of her book *Editing for Directors,* Gael Chandler compares writing a book to making a film, just as we are comparing crafting a sermon to making a film:

> You begin with a concept of a golden narrative that reaches people and makes a difference. You research, ponder and plan—preproduction. You start production, writing, and find yourself slogging through doubts, blocks, and turn downs, along with new discoveries, joys, connections, and the satisfaction of completing another section. Then you edit—move sections around, delete sentences, expand others. At all times, the project is never far from your mind. Finally, you send it in and let it go, accepting what it has become and hoping your intentions for your audience or readers will be realized.[37]

36. Murch, *Blink of an Eye*, 15.

37. Gael Chandler, *Editing for Directors: A Guide for Creative Collaboration* (Studio City, CA: Michael Wiese Productions, 2021), xi.

6

Fade Out: Creating the Closing

"Everyone. Everything. Everywhere. Ends." Thus read HBO's poster for the final season of *Six Feet Under,* a series centered on a family of morticians. Its finale delivered as promised: viewers found out how each character met their death. While few TV series or movies conclude with every character dying, many a show has sent us off satisfied with the ending, however expected or surprising. The ending makes clear that the world set out in the opening has changed, or at least shifted, and shows how much or little the characters have changed.

No other part of the sermon has a lasting impact like its closing minutes. While that lasting impact depends on what happens in the beginning and the middle, as long as your hearers have stuck with the sermon, it's those last minutes they'll remember. Even then they may not remember what was said, or even what the theme was, they will likely remember what their experience was, what they were feeling.

The confusion over how to close a sermon often results in an abrupt ending. Just as commonly, there are too many endings when one ending is sufficient. The goal is not to summarize the whole sermon; imagine the futility of a film doing a rapid time lapse through the whole film or the director stepping out on screen to explain all that happened. Just as the ending of an impactful film might aim to get the conversation started, so might a sermon closing.

Given the undeniable significance of and the stubborn problems with sermon closings, much advice has been offered, including "tell them what you said" after you've told them what you're going to say and then told them. Or, "sit down in the storm" after "start low, go slow, climb higher, strike fire."[1] Many preachers say, "I always leave them with a concrete call to action." What advice have you heard? What advice do you heed?

In the same way that you were invited in chapter 3 to review a few of your own sermon openings, take some time now to review the closings of a few of your sermons. Try to describe what you do. Do you . . . .

—summarize the main point(s) of the sermon?
—assure the congregation with a bold gospel proclamation?
—encourage the congregation to accept Jesus's invitation to follow him?
—exhort the people to live their lives differently?

Take this exploration a level deeper by articulating *why* you do what you do. What is the effect you desire? Some preachers' primary goal in the closing of the sermon is to leave people with a sense of hope. Others give a clear list of shoulds and musts so that there is no question about how to live as a disciple of Jesus. Others want to leave hearers with a zinger in the form of a question: So, what will you do? Still others want their hearers to be comforted with the assurance that God is present in their grief.

Sermon closings, like film endings, do not produce themselves. They deserve careful attention in order to meet the objective. Do you want your hearers to know something? Feel something? Do something? You will need to revise until the *what* and the *why* align.

ON VARIETY

If you always do the same thing, it's time to mix it up. Do so not just for the sake of variety but to match the sermon objective, which changes depending on the occasion, the Scripture reading, events in the community or in the world. As the objective changes, so does the way to achieve that objective. Repeating the same thing to achieve different results is not effective.

1. William C. Turner Jr., "The Musicality of Black Preaching," in *Performance in Preaching: Bringing the Sermon to Life*, ed. Jana Childers and Clayton Schmit (Grand Rapids: Baker Academic Press, 2008), 191.

Consider the variety in the endings of the four Gospels:

— Matthew: The resurrected Jesus assures the disciples of his ongoing presence as he commissions them to go into the world to baptize and teach (28:18–20).
— Luke: The resurrected Jesus blesses the disciples before ascending to heaven, prompting them to joyfully return to Jerusalem to bless God in the temple (24:50–53).
— John: The crowds thin as the book closes. Jesus appears to the disciples. Then the narrative zooms in to Jesus and Peter before focusing solely on the Beloved Disciple. "This is the disciple who is testifying to these things and has written them, and we know that his testimony is true. But there are also many other things that Jesus did; if every one of them were written down, I suppose that the world itself could not contain the books that would be written" (21:24–25).
— Mark: The oldest of the four Gospels has three possible endings. The first is 16:8, "So they went out and fled from the tomb, for terror and amazement had seized them; and they said nothing to anyone, for they were afraid." The "they" here is three women, Mary Magdalene, Mary the mother of James, and Salome. The powers that be (or were) could not accept the fear and silence of this ending, so they appended more satisfying endings. The shorter ending reintroduces Peter and Jesus and emphasizes the ubiquitous proclamation of salvation. In the longer ending, verses 9–20, Jesus appears first to Mary Magdalene, then to two disciples, before commissioning all the disciples, then ascending. The longer ending closes with the disciples proclaiming the good news to the world. Some manuscripts add "Amen." (More on that word later.)

Endings matter. Possibilities abound. Variety makes things interesting. Likely you appreciate multiple film genres, though you might have a favorite. Likely too, the films and television shows you love do not all end in the same way. Test this claim for yourself. Revisit the last four or five minutes of your favorite films and television shows. Do they offer you a new idea? Do they engage your emotions? Do they motivate you to some kind of behavior?

Varying the closings of your sermons does not mean jettisoning what you've been doing; it just means broadening your repertoire of possible ways to close a sermon. Doing so may leave you a bit outside your comfort zone, but remember that doing so is for your hearers, not yourself. Screenwriter Michael Arndt (*Little Miss Sunshine, Toy Story 3*) says that after all the "selfish work" of the first drafts of a screenplay, which are written for oneself, one has to pivot toward the audience. "You are not making your film for yourself."[2] That's good advice for preachers too.

How does one choose an ending, for a film or for a sermon, that offers the viewer or hearer the desired experience? The variety of film endings and their objectives can help preachers expand their repertoire for crafting those important last minutes.

TYPES OF ENDINGS

Filmmakers conclude their shows in three basic ways. They use a *closed ending* (most common in the United States), an *open ending* (most common in other locations, including Australia, Asia, and Europe), or a *hybrid ending* that is a combination of the two (most common in TV).[3]

—A closed ending ties up all the knots, making clear how the story ends and giving closure to its characters. It resolves all the conflicts and answers all the viewers' questions. For instance, a closed ending leaves no doubt that the peace has been won, the couple has tied the knot (another allusion to tying up the plot), the child has been born, the family has come to terms with their grief, and so on. While a closed ending can be expected or formulaic, it is definitive, leaving little room for debate or interpretation. Film example: *Judas and the Black Messiah* (2021) leaves no doubt as to the fates of Black Panther Chairman Fred Hampton and his FBI informant betrayer.

—An open ending leaves the audience with a question or a bunch of questions: Did the hero live or get killed or deliberately disappear? What actually happened at the end? Where exactly did the hero or villain end up? Open endings can leave viewers

2. Meg LeFauve and Lorien McKenna, "Michael Arndt's Act 1 Masterclass (Rebroadcast)," episode 165 of *The Screenwriting Life with Meg LeFauve and Lorien McKenna* (podcast), 5:50, November 16, 2023, https://podcasts.apple .com/us/podcast/the-screenwriting-life-with-meg-lefauve-and-lorien-mckenna /id1501641442?i=1000635043781.

3. Christopher Vogler, *The Writer's Journey: Mythic Structure for Writers* (Studio City, CA: Michael Wiese Productions, 2020), 250.

reflecting and drawing their own moral conclusions, conversing with others, or creating the ending themselves in their minds or through their actions. Documentaries about social issues or history often leave the ending to the audience to act on. A cliff-hanger is a prime example of an open ending. Film example: *The Sopranos* series concluded in 2007 with a cut to black, an ambiguous ending that left viewers debating whether Tony's enemies were closing in to whack him or he was simply going to enjoy a family meal in a diner.

— Hybrid endings answer some questions but leave others open. TV series routinely employ this type of ending to keep viewers tuning in to the next episode or season by tying up some plotlines and finishing off some characters while introducing new characters and conflicts. They also use cliff-hangers, as do movie series, which look to sequels for a continuing revenue stream. Film example: Serial movies with hybrid endings have been around since silent movies, such as *The Perils of Pauline* (1914).

Script consultant Christopher Vogler writes in *The Writer's Journey* that every story should end like a sentence with a punctuation mark (PM), reflective of the filmmaker's desired impact on the audience.[4]

PM	Description of Ending	Film Example
.	Ending with period is akin to making a definitive statement and constitutes a closed ending.	Both *Butch Cassidy and the Sundance Kid* (1969) and *Thelma and Louise* (1991) sent their on-the-run duos to their deaths, finishing with a freeze-frame and leaving no doubt as to their fates.
?	Ending with a question mark clearly is an open ending and throws it to the audience to decide and discuss.	With its linear story line filmed in black-and-white and its reverse chronological story line shot in color, *Memento* (2000) left moviegoers ruminating on what happened at the end due to the protagonist's unreliable memory and his wife's murder remaining unsolved.

continued on next page

4. Vogler, *Writer's Journey*, 261.

PM	Description of Ending (cont.)	Film Example (cont.)
!	Ending with an exclamation point—a hybrid ending—creates an emphatic and clear conclusion yet sounds an alarm, challenging the audience to write the final ending (as ending with an ellipsis can also do). It can ask, Will the historical truth be told? Will the right be wronged, the problem solved?	The documentary *An Inconvenient Truth* (2006) laid out the impending doom of global warming and provided preventative actions moviegoers could take.
. . .	Ending with an ellipsis—also a hybrid ending—brings mystery and says, "To be continued . . ." The continuation may take the form of a sequel, next week's TV episode, or a challenge to the audience.	The sci-fi flick *Invasion of the Body Snatchers* (1956 and its 1978 remake) gave a metaphorical warning of the dangers of parasitic pod people—soulless conformists—taking over the United States. *The Teachers' Lounge* (2023) ends elliptically, leaving the audience debating the thief's identity and the future for the teacher, her brightest student, and schooling.

It might be said that most sermon endings are hybrid since they often proclaim at once the good news of Jesus's death and resurrection and prompt hearers to consider, Now what? They could be closed when the preacher leaves no doubt about the unmerited, liberative grace of God. A sermon ending could be considered open when it does not resolve questions, leaving it up to the hearers how they might act in the world as people free *from* proving themselves worthy to God and free *for* serving the neighbor and all of God's creation. Vogler's taxonomy is helpful here to determine what kind of sermon ending to employ.

PM	Type of Ending	Description of Ending	Sermon Example and Occasion
.	Closed	Ending with a period is akin to making a definitive statement or a proclamation.	A sermon that closes with a gospel proclamation that leaves no doubt as to where one stands with God. • Possible occasion: Easter Sunday
?	Open	Ending with a question mark throws it to the hearers to decide and discuss.	Sometimes sermons literally end with a question, leaving the choice of how things will turn out on the conscience of the individual or a community. • Possible occasion: a prophetic sermon that critiques the church's failure to live as the body of Christ and invites or exhorts the church to change. At other times, the last statement(s) may not be interrogatory, but it leaves something unresolved. • Possible occasion: Good Friday
!	Hybrid	Ending with an exclamation point creates an emphatic and clear conclusion yet sounds an alarm. It can ask, Will the historical truth be told? Will the right be wronged, the problem solved?	• Possible occasion: Easter Sunday or funeral
...	Hybrid	Ending with an ellipsis brings mystery and says, "To be continued . . ." The continuation may take the form of a sequel or a challenge to the audience.	A sermon that invites the congregation to finish the story or is part of a sermon series on a particular topic or theme. • Possible occasion: Palm Sunday

Which punctuation mark best represents your most recent sermon closing? Perhaps an example will help. Consider Barack Obama's eulogy for the Rev. Clementa Pinckney on June 26, 2015.[5] State Senator Pinckney and eight parishioners, together now called the Emanuel Nine, were shot and killed by a gunman as they were meeting for Bible study at Emanuel AME Church in Charleston, South Carolina. Nine days later, Obama leads up to the climax of his nearly thirty-eight-minute eulogy in this way:

> Clem understood that justice grows out of recognition of ourselves in each other; that my liberty depends on you being free, too. [applause] That—that that history can't be a sword to justify injustice or a shield against progress. It must be a manual for how to avoid repeating the mistakes of the past, how to break the cycle, a roadway toward a better world. He knew that the path of grace involves an open mind. But more importantly, an open heart. That's what I felt this week—an open heart. That more than any particular policy or analysis is what's called upon right now, I think. It's what a friend of mine, the writer Marilyn Robinson, calls "that reservoir of goodness beyond and of another kind, that we are able to do each other in the ordinary cause of things." That reservoir of goodness. If we can find that grace, anything is possible. [applause]
> [34:58]

Here, Obama slows his pace and pauses regularly. The congregation fills those silences as they audibly add to the sermon.

> If we can tap that grace, everything can change. Amazing grace, amazing grace. [silence]

Then, Obama is silent for a full thirteen seconds. The next thing out of his mouth is not speaking but singing.

> [35:32] (singing) Amazing grace . . . [singing, applause, the crowd rising]
> . . . how sweet the sound that saved a wretch like me. I once was lost, but now I'm found, was blind, but now, I see. [applause]

5. "Transcript: Obama Delivers Eulogy for Charleston Pastor, the Rev. Clementa Pinckney," *Washington Post,* June 26, 2015, https://www.washingtonpost.com/news/post-nation/wp/2015/06/26/transcript-obama-delivers-eulogy-for-charleston-pastor-the-rev-clementa-pinckney/.

The then president and the congregation take a full minute to sing that one verse before Obama continues.

> [36:35] Clementa Pinckney found that grace . . . [applause]
> Cynthia Hurd found that grace . . . [applause]
> Susie Jackson found that grace . . . [applause]
> Ethel Lance found that grace . . . [applause]
> DePayne Middleton-Doctor found that grace . . . [applause]
> Tywanza Sanders found that grace . . . [applause]
> Daniel L. Simmons, Sr., found that grace . . . [applause]
> Sharonda Coleman-Singleton found that grace . . . [applause]
> Myra Thompson found that grace . . . [applause]
> . . . through the example of their lives. They've now passed it onto us. May we find ourselves worthy of that precious and extraordinary gift as long as our lives endure. May grace now lead them home. May God continue to shed His Grace on the United States of America.

"Celebration," a term distinctively used to describe Black preaching in the United States, "is characterized by content that affirms the goodness and powerful intervention of God as well as style that builds from quiet beginnings to an emotionally rich crescendo in conclusion."[6] The singing and the anaphora (repeated "found that grace") are the climax of Obama's funeral sermon. The sermon ending is "closed" in terms of getting the congregation to that "celebration" of God's amazing grace; there is no doubt in the preacher's announcement that God has graced and blessed these people. And yet all who gathered knew it wasn't the end of things. The Rev. Clementa Pinckney's loved ones still grieved, and a nation still grieves racially motivated gun violence.

The brief *denouement* that follows the climax, a common threefold "may," opens things back up again as it asks, Will we learn this time? Whether the example of the lives of the Emanuel Nine will "find ourselves worthy of that precious and extraordinary gift as long as our lives endure" remains to be seen. Because of this mix of being closed and open, the sermon ending is hybrid as it closes, as noted above, with an exclamation point that creates an emphatic and clear conclusion yet sounds an alarm, challenging the audience to write the final ending.

---

6. Cleophus LaRue, *Rethinking Celebration: From Rhetoric to Praise in African American Preaching* (Louisville, KY: Westminster John Knox Press, 2016), back cover.

OBJECTIVES OF ENDINGS

The ecstatic experience of being caught up in the celebration of God's amazing grace will eventually simmer and give way to a different reality of God's grace in the world. The transition can be disorienting. Similarly, how many times have we sat in a theater as the movie ended and the lights came up and felt momentarily disoriented, then sad to be taken out of the world we were embedded in? Well-done film endings affect us in this way. They can also leave us cognizant that our questions have been answered as plotlines have been fulfilled, characters reached a believable destiny, and the story achieved its final, cumulative impact. While viewers may not see an ending coming (all the better!), when an ending does its job, they accept it as fitting when it is in keeping with the film's promise and foreshadowing. A felicitous ending resolves the mystery and answers the central question raised in the show's opening scenes while aligning with the logline and advertising (as laid out in chap. 1).

First and foremost, a show's ending must fulfill the filmmaker's desired impact. Vogler writes, "A story is like a weaving in which the characters are interwoven into a coherent design. The plot lines are knotted together to create conflict and tension, and usually it's desirable to release the tension and resolve the conflicts by untying these knots."[7] The ending of a film follows its *climax* or *anticlimax* and is the denouement (French for "the untying" or "unknotting"). Denouement shows up in other narrative mediums, such as literature, where it originated, podcasts, . . . and sermons!

In addition to unraveling and thereby tying up the plot, a film denouement can set up an audience for a sequel or a prequel. A TV episode can neatly tie up a drama, comedy situation, case, or mystery, or create a cliff-hanger, leaving the viewer yearning for the next episode (or bingeing the entire series). Many episodes do both: They solve the crises of the episode and generate fresh problems for their characters to wrangle with in future episodes. Does this mean that a good ending is happy, tidy, or totally clear? Not at all. A successful ending can leave us with a host of different thoughts and feelings and motivations. In both filmmaking and preaching, any one of the three types of endings (open, closed, hybrid) can aim to impact the audience in terms of cognition, emotion, or action.

---

7. Vogler, *Writer's Journey*, 250.

Next, we'll identify how film endings achieve each type of impact and make some recommendations for how sermon endings can do the same.

To Know (Cognitive Impact)

Most films do not exist simply to give information. So, too, with sermons . . . ideally. For many centuries, preaching was akin to rhetoric, with a primary aim of persuading the congregation to assent to a certain belief. Perhaps this had to do with preserving hierarchical systems by limiting access to information. The preacher had information that the people in the pew did not until and unless the preacher would share it. In today's internet age, however, access to information (e.g., the Bible translated into one's own language) is not an obstacle for as many people. While sermons do often teach, this more traditional style of preaching cannot be assumed and is perhaps less desired these days, since sermons tend to "preach to the choir," meaning they aim "to inspire [their] supporters rather than persuade [their] detractors."[8] As one writer says, "Most of our gospel proclamation is rather pedestrian, evoking philosophical ideas and arguments but not much of anything else. It doesn't stick because it doesn't demand much from our imagination, our hearts, and our souls. But the gospel message is so much more than just cognitive acquiescence to propositional truth."[9]

Preachers do often want hearers to know things such as "you are loved" or "despite your doubts or even your unfaithfulness, God's grace is sufficient" or "the Bible is not just an ancient text, it's your book of life too." Even so, the aim of knowing these things is to feel, to have an experience. Here is where preachers can wholeheartedly take a cue from filmmakers who know that whether the final image is scary, soothing, revelatory, enigmatic, or something else, it should pack an emotional punch.

8. As noted by writer Rebecca Solnit, who called Martin Luther King Jr.'s "I Have a Dream" speech "an example of preaching to the choir at its best." Solnit, "Preaching to the Choir," *Harper's,* November 2017. Solnit notes that "conversion or the transmission of new information is not the primary aim; the preacher has other work to do."

9. Soong-Chan Rah, foreword to *Fear Not! A Christian Appreciation of Horror Movies,* by Josh Larsen (Eugene, OR: Cascade, 2023), x.

To Feel (Emotional Impact)

Screenwriter Michael Arndt emphasizes emotional impact: "You remember a handful of scenes and you remember how [the movie] made you feel. . . . My goal is not to articulate an idea. My goal is to create a feeling that the audience has when they walk out of the theatre because that's what they will remember."[10] Whether utilizing a closed, open, or hybrid ending, filmmakers pay much attention to the emotional impact the ending will have on their audience.

Filmmakers create happy endings to leave the audience content, for example, to see lovers finally united (*Moonlight*, 2016), villains getting satisfying punishments (*Inglorious Basterds*, 2009), and characters reconciling with their past (*Nebraska*, 2013). The final episode of the comedy series *Schitt's Creek*, "Happy Ending" (2020), propelled the Rose family out of their motel toward a rosy future and earned writing, directing, and cast Emmys. A variation of the happy ending is the upbeat ending that leaves the protagonist, along with the audience, at peace. *A Man Called Otto* (2022) faded out with Otto dying, having come to terms with his wife's death and his new and old neighbors, composing an ending that brings hope after suffering. The documentary *Every Body* (2023) tempered the medical maltreatment, public shame, and personal stories of intersex individuals by ending with optimistic scenes of intersex people and their allies in different countries demonstrating publicly for ethical, consensual medical treatment.

A sad, bittersweet, or tragic ending can be powerfully impactful as it elicits deep emotions and is perceived as realistic and believable. Audiences often trust sad endings, finding them true to life (*Just Mercy*, 2019) as characters suffer for their actions (*Glory*, 1989) or are the victims of others' actions (*The Boy in the Striped Pajamas*, 2008). Sad endings can help viewers deal with loss, grief, death, trauma, crime, injustice, mental illness—the many tough parts of life. Family and couple partings abound in tearjerkers such as *Gypsy* (1962) and *Brokeback Mountain* (2005). *Bambi* (1942), *Old Yeller* (1957), and *Bridge to Terabithia* (2007) helped children deal with death. Tragedy can make for reflection, catharsis, conversation, learning, or a desire for change. Based on a true story, *Boys Don't Cry* (1999) increased

10. Meg LeFauve and Lorien McKenna, "Michael Arndt's Act 1 Masterclass (Rebroadcast)," episode 165 of *The Screenwriting Life with Meg LeFauve and Lorien McKenna* (podcast), 51:50, November 16, 2023, https://podcasts.apple .com/us/podcast/the-screenwriting-life-with-meg-lefauve-and-lorien-mckenna /id1501641442?i=1000635043781.

awareness of transgender people's struggles and vulnerabilities as it detailed the life of a young transgender man who was raped and murdered. Sacrifice (noble and unintentional) also plays a part in sad endings. At the end of *Casablanca* (1942), Rick lets his beloved Ilsa fly away with her Nazi-hunted husband, claiming, "The problems of three little people don't amount to a hill of beans in this crazy world."

Film endings are not only happy or sad. They also have the power to shock, terrify, motivate, invigorate, discombobulate. Filmmakers work diligently to achieve emotional impact in their films. Just as films are more complex than simply happy endings or sad endings, so are sermons. They can do more than, as the saying goes, comfort the afflicted or afflict the comfortable. While not all emotional possibilities for film endings are appropriate for sermon endings, for the gospel to take hold in our hearers we need to be specific in planning for a sermon's emotional impact.

Even if people cannot describe the sermon ending in detail, we hope they might be able to describe what they felt. As an experiment (and perhaps as the start of a routine), ask some people to pay close attention to how they feel at the close of your sermon. Don't get too discouraged if you encounter resistance. Somehow people have gotten the sense that some feelings are not welcome at church, so they do not acknowledge them. Asking these same people what happened to them when they saw a recent film or television show will likely yield quick responses. Somehow, they can readily name an emotion triggered by TV and film. Perhaps some people are of the mind that tapping into feelings is considered weak and therefore are unable to name (perhaps even experience) the gamut of emotions.

In other words, preachers may have some equipping to do. They can assist hearers with emotional literacy (the ability to name and communicate feelings) and help them understand that bringing their whole selves to worship is acceptable. Offering some possibilities, such as those listed below, might help.

After hearing your sermon, I felt . . .

Calm	Scared	Motivated	Empowered
Humbled	Happy	Vindicated	Anxious
Surprised	Sad	Challenged	Jealous
Confused	Expectant	Accepted	Relaxed
Disgusted	Angry	Amazed	Annoyed
Bored	Hopeful	Relieved	Eager

_____ (fill in the blank)

If you are thinking all this talk about feelings is fluffy, you may be in good company. But you're certainly not in the company of filmmakers who insist, as filmmaker Jason Wilkinson does, "Apathy is our worst enemy. . . . Above all, I'm trying to make an audience feel something."[11] The repertoire of those feelings is much broader than happy, sad, or scared.

Perhaps we've gotten ahead of ourselves. Preachers, do you know what emotional impact you are hoping for with your sermon? If you're not sure about that, chances are your hearers will not be able to express what they felt either. They would likely choose "confused" from the list above. Since the close of the sermon is where you "bring it home," you will want to be clear about the lasting impression you want to make (remember the function statement) and double-check that the sermon closing has the best possible opportunity to generate that emotional impact.

This isn't to say every feeling at the end of a sermon will be cheerful or welcomed. After all, the gospel is indeed a scandal: money changers' tables get overturned, Jesus makes friends with the outcast and marginalized, dead people are said to rise again. The Bible is no Hallmark movie. But just as a film ending that isn't happy "can be powerfully impactful as it elicits deep emotions and is perceived as realistic and believable," as noted above, so, too,— can sermons.

There are some feelings that preachers do not want their hearers to feel. One example, confusion, has already been mentioned. Confusion happens when preachers (a) start a whole new topic in the last few minutes, (b) undermine what they said earlier, or (c) suddenly lose energy and focus, leaving the sermon to peter out or just . . . well, end. Another unwelcome feeling is frustration. One of the biggest frustrations for hearers is when a preacher starts to descend but fails to land the plane, so to speak, then ascends for another revolution around the airport. Preachers don't typically get encores, but some take them anyway in the form of multiple—effectively too many—endings. This frustrates hearers just as much as a speaker who notes they have three points to make and after the third says, "And now to my fourth point . . ."

Confusion and frustration are preventable if preachers avoid the pitfalls named in the previous paragraph—pitfalls that also plague filmmakers. Many of us have left the cinema feeling let down by a movie's ending, complaining, "That doesn't make sense" or "They would never

11. Author (Hannan) conversation with Wilkinson, March 27, 2018.

do that." Sometimes we feel duped, as when the ending of *The Village* (2004) reveals that the nineteenth-century villagers menaced by monsters are just modern-day folks in costumes. A good movie with a proper setup and characters can have a poor ending by failing to follow through with a worthy conclusion, succumbing to convention, or not trusting its characters or audience. Problem endings can be rewritten or reshot, assuming the budget is there, or played with in editing, especially if there are too many endings. An example of too many endings might be the 2023 film *I Am a Noise* (2023). Ostensibly the life story of Joan Baez, it's neither a concert film (no song is completely sung and singing does not dominate the emotional aspects) nor a traditional biopic. Rather, it's the life journey of a soul—more of a memoir—and Baez is the primary storyteller. It could have ended with the last song of her final concert tour but instead goes out with her wandering her land and dancing, having mostly made peace with the dark undercurrents of her life.

Appealing to emotions in the sermon closing need not mean preachers are being manipulative (the sermon should respect the whole person) or dumbing down (the sermon should be thoughtfully logical). It really comes down to where you want to leave the story and your audience. The emotional impact occurs as a result of something having changed. In films, whether the ending is closed, open, or hybrid, something has to have changed by the end. Similarly, no sermon is preached to maintain the status quo. Has the reversal in a biblical figure's character sparked a change in our own journey? Has our sense of who God is changed? How are we affected emotionally by these changes? The hope is that people walk out into the world at least feeling something other than apathetic.

To Do (Behavioral Impact)

Behavior change is a goal of some filmmakers. Chapter 1 introduced film impact teams, which continue the work of the film once it's viewed to assist audiences in making an impact in the world. In response to a letter from a viewer complaining that the violence in *Straw Dogs* made the film impossible to enjoy, director Sam Peckinpah said, "I didn't want you to enjoy the film, I wanted you to look very close at your own soul."[12] Writer Scott Tobias notes, "Stepping away from the Western genre for the first time, Peckinpah directly confronts the violence at the heart of masculinity; as his response to the letter-writer implies, he wanted men to consider the unsettling extent to which it defines their actions."[13] Recognition is a first step toward change.

When one thinks of films that lead to a change in behavior, one thinks of documentaries. Documentaries often unapologetically aim for behavioral transformation. Recall Don Schwartz's claim that "documentary filmmakers are liberators" and Jeff Skoll's "different kind of philanthropy" that is willing to risk losing money as long as "the good that comes from [the film] outweighs the risk." The tagline for the company Films for Good is "Good People Doing Good."[14] Another example is Odyssey Networks, which is

> a multi-faith multi-media non-profit that brings together organizations and individuals around powerful programming that supports people of all faiths and good will as they engage the world to nurture compassion, justice and hope. We give faith a voice in the public square, showing the civic value of faith in action. . . . Odyssey's programs encourage people of faith and good will to work together and take action towards making the world a better place for all humankind. We build impact campaigns that bring together coalitions of faith-based and secular change-makers to address some of the most pressing social issues facing our world.[15]

Films need not be so *on the nose* with their intentions as if it were the cinematic equivalent to an altar call. Genres other than documentary also aim for behavior change, if more subtly. Often religious films end with a moral, yes. Yet other kinds of drama focus on redemption, life choices, righting wrongs, overcoming adversity, and teaching life lessons, such as overcoming self-doubt or bigotry. Revenge movies can center on righting wrongs—personal wrongs as in the two *Kill Bill* movies (2003–4) or societal wrongs as in *Promising Young Woman* (2020). Movies about redemption include Oscar-winning *Schindler's List*

12. Sam Peckinpah quoted in Scott Tobias, "Straw Dogs," AV Club, April 8, 2003, https://www.avclub.com/straw-dogs-1798198413.

13. Tobias, "Straw Dogs."

14. Films for Good, https://filmsforgood.com.

15. "Our Mission," Odyssey Networks, http://www.odysseynetworks.org. See also Journey Films, https://www.journeyfilms.com/about.

(1993) about factory owner Oskar Schindler, who kept twelve hundred Jews from extermination, and *The Shawshank Redemption* (1994), in which two prison inmates become best friends. These films seek not only to tell a story but also to inspire analogous behaviors in the audience.

Moral endings continue to be seen in superhero movies—both animated and live action—where superheroes singly (*Batman, Black Panther, Wonder Woman*) and collectively (*The Incredibles, Justice League, The Avengers*) fight righteous battles for the welfare of others. Sometimes the moral is clear—the goal accomplished, the lesson learned, the journey completed. For example, the protagonist in *Precious* (2007) overcomes parental sexual abuse and abandonment to move toward a better life with her children. At other times, the character achieves a Pyrrhic victory or there is no good choice or the whole quest is questionable. In *Sophie's Choice* (1982), Sophie has to choose between two lovers, one representing life and sanity, the other death and madness. Unable to escape her guilt from a Nazi-forced choice over which of her two children would survive Auschwitz, she opts for death.

These kinds of films and the powerful ways in which they end have the capacity to change individual and societal behaviors even without offering an explicit demand or exhortation at the end. Given sermons' unfortunate reputation for being "preachy," preachers can learn from filmmakers in this way. While this isn't the volume to tease out the rhetorical nuances of sermon closings, it is worth noting that the indicative mood ("We are disciples") can be more impactful in shaping behavior than the imperative mood ("Be a disciple") or the interrogative mood ("Are you a disciple?"). The advantages of the indicative mood are many. It offers a chance for the final word to be good news that prioritizes God's action in Jesus to free individuals from having to prove their worth through their actions. This freedom is not carte blanche to behave destructively without repercussion but to be freed *for* caring for others and, indeed, the whole of creation. Life is about shoulds and musts in order to earn our keep, our reputations, our self-worth. We go to church for something different. When we are drowning in shoulds and musts, it is difficult actually to attend to them, even if we know that we should and must. Good news can be motivating.

The indicative mood also offers hearers space to ruminate in order to come to their own conclusion and perhaps change their behavior. Churchgoers should be as free to respond and come to their own conclusions—maybe even transformations—as moviegoers are. Preaching has benefited from its long-standing conversation with the discipline of performance studies and its work on "aesthetic distance." In his book, *Distance in Preaching*, Michael Brothers writes, "Distance encourages and protects the responses of the hearer (emotions, criticism, passions, thoughts, judgments, rejections, and acceptances) as integral to the performance."[16] Consider this: if people do not appreciate films that speak down to viewers with on-the-nose moralism, why would they welcome being told what to do in a sermon? As another homiletician argues, "Sermons that employ distancing devices and techniques give the hearer room, or space, to consider a message without being lured, pressured, manipulated, or coerced by means of direct confrontation. The result of maintaining distance is free participation in the Christian message."[17]

Imagine the impact when preachers equip hearers to recognize the subtext of sermons and then trust them. Filmgoers certainly have grown savvy from watching films for over a century and a quarter now. They understand and speak film lingo—close-up, flashback, mismatch, and so on. They readily read actors' faces, anticipate plotlines, spot *Easter eggs* and *CGI* (computer-generated images), and converse about upcoming shows, series, and remakes.

So how do films pull off being less preachy while still resulting in some impactful behavioral changes? They use a variety of ending techniques, and so can preachers.

OTHER ENDING TECHNIQUES

Surprise Endings, a.k.a. Twist Endings

Barbie director and cowriter Greta Gerwig wanted a "'mic drop' moment to bring the movie to a close."[18] The film's final line, "I'm here to see my gynecologist," both honors Barbie's inventor Ruth

16. Michael Brothers, *Distance in Preaching: Room to Speak, Space to Listen* (Grand Rapids: Wm. B. Eerdmans Publishing Co., 2014), 44.

17. Mason Lee, "Vulnerable Good News: Distance and Patience in Gospel Performance" (presentation, Academy of Homiletics Annual Meeting, Dallas, TX, 2017).

18. Gerwig revealed that her closing line came to her in a dream. Jazmin Tolliver, "Greta Gerwig Reveals What Sparked the 'Mic-Drop' Ending of 'Barbie,'" *Huffington Post*, July 26, 2023, https://www.huffpost.com/entry/greta-gerwig-reveals-what-sparked-barbies-mic-drop-ending_n_64c137e8e4b093f07cb6ab04.

Handler and offers an empowering "body-positive message to young girls." Gerwig hopes behaviors will change.[19]

This ending is a surprising twist that does not feel like a patronizing, "and here, boys and girls, is the moral of the story." It seems like a closed ending in which the loose ends are tied up, but the hoped-for impact in the world remains to be seen. Barbie has become human, but have we become humane? So, again, we have a hybrid ending.[20]

While not every sermon needs to nor should aim for a mic drop finish, such endings can have a powerful impact. One example is a sermon based on Matthew 3:1–12 in which the preacher opened with a detailed description about a young woman in deep anguish.[21]

> Melissa sits in a fetal position on her kitchen floor. It is the middle of the night and she has crumbled to the floor after standing looking through a small break in the blinds for almost two hours. She has been high for days and is married to a man who controls her every move, beats her, sexually abuses her, and gives her dope. So she stays.
>
> She is desperate. She is spiritually bankrupt.
>   And she is in the wilderness,
>   a wilderness born out of a need to escape the pain.
>
>   A feeling that she belongs nowhere,
>   an understanding that she is meant for nothing.
>   A need to be numb and stay numb and not feel all the things.

The preacher then offers the start of a twist ("But . . .") before referring to a wilderness story in Scripture.

> But that night on the kitchen floor she felt something, something that somehow she knew was there all along—God's loving spirit enveloping her.

19. Greg Evans, "Greta Gerwig Explains Barbie's 'Mic Drop' Final Line," July 24, 2023, https://deadline.com/tag/ruth-handler/.

20. Scott Tobias, review of *Barbie,* Reveal, July 20, 2023. "The battle of the sexes rages on in 2023, just as it did when Ruth Handler created the doll in 1959, and Gerwig makes it clear that nothing has been settled."

21. Shared by permission of Amy Sperline Walls.

> Like arms around her that she could simply not bear to turn into.
> Like glimpses of the sun bouncing off of the Jordan river.

> The wilderness in the gospel story is also a place for the
> marginalized.

With this transition, the preacher shifts the focus of the sermon to John the Baptist in the wilderness and the transformation that is possible when people show up for others in Jesus's name. She then asks the congregation, "In what ways are we curled up in a ball on the floor? Afraid to dip into the life-giving waters that we know are there but refuse to acknowledge?" Here the preacher offers room for hearers to identify with Melissa. Eventually she invites them to consider identifying with those who show up for others. "How will we respond? How *are* we responding?" She continues:

> I see the cleansing that John is performing as the place in
> which I must place myself, figuratively, for all those who live
> their lives in and amongst my own and be the glimmer of
> hope bouncing off of the Jordan like beams of sunlight in the
> darkness. Be the one who can say

> THIS IS THE TIME FOR YOU TO LIVE INTO THE CLEANS-
> ING NATURE OF GOD'S LOVE FOR YOU. I SEE THE FRUIT
> WITHIN YOU, THE FRUIT THAT YOU WILL BEAR IN YOUR
> LIFE!!

> THIS IS YOUR TIME.

And with that she moves toward proclaiming the climax of the sermon:

> The power, the gift of Jesus Christ is here. It is here, it is ever
> present in our lives, and it is always reaching out for us. Let
> us learn each day to live wet in the cleansing waters of bap-
> tism, in the purification of our Lord, and
> let us be disciples to those who are just like us,
> wandering in and out of the wilderness.

Ending here would be fitting and perhaps lead to some kind of behavioral change. However, the preacher rightly intuits that the emotional impact of the opening story about Melissa calls for a reprise. And so she adds:

If you are wondering about Melissa, whether or not she
found her way out of the wilderness?? I can offer this to you . . .
she stands before you,
living in the hope found in the Grace that we are all offered
and that was given to us without strings attached,
symbolized in the cross where Jesus died for us,
for all of us.

This sermon closing offers a twist that rings out because it rings true. "Stories in service to the gospel need to have gravitas worthy of the subject matter of humanity's deepest concern and God's expansive care for the world."[22] In the roundtable discussion after the sermon, hearers affirmed how the sermon acknowledged both the realities of being human and the expansiveness of God's care for the world. Indeed, "for congregations to experience God's good news in an *emotional* and transformational way, the good news in sermons needs to be shown to be true to their lives."[23]

Of course, the preacher could have opened the sermon by telling the hearers that this is her story. But that decision may have made the hearers overfocus on the preacher with sympathy, thereby missing the broader point. Also, such an opening would have been far less cathartic. As David Buttrick writes, "Destruction of suspense (the possibility of the unexpected) is positively unkind."[24] Wes Allen and Carrie La Ferle put it this way: "Sermonic stories need something *unexpected* to be sticky."[25] Preachers might ask of their ending, "Would the climax and resolution offer a twist that is unexpected and inviting while ringing credible and desirable to the listeners?"[26]

A surprise ending is the ultimate *plot twist* as it brings the film to a close in a way that the audience didn't anticipate. The host of NPR's *Hidden Brain*, Shankar Vedantam, remarked on a show titled "A Conversation about Life's Unseen Patterns,"

22. O. Wesley Allen, Jr. and Carrie La Ferle, *Preaching and the Thirty-Second Commercial: Lessons from Advertising for the Pulpit* (Louisville, KY: Westminster John Knox Press, 2021), 94.

23. Allen and La Ferle, *Preaching and the Commercial*, 95.

24. David Buttrick, *Homiletic: Moves and Structures* (Minneapolis: Fortress Press, 1987), 85.

25. Allen and La Ferle, *Preaching and the Commercial*, 94.

26. Allen and La Ferle, *Preaching and the Commercial*, 96.

Writers and filmmakers hoping to hoodwink their fans with plot twists have long known what cognitive scientists know: All of us have blind spots in the way we assess the world. We get distracted. We forget how we know things. We see patterns that aren't there. Because these blind spots are wired into the brain, they act in ways that are predictable—so predictable that storytellers from Sophocles to M. Night Shyamalan have used them to lead us astray.[27]

To pull off a surprise ending, filmmakers must not be arbitrary or just think it's a cool idea. Rather, they must stay true to the plot and characters they've focused on for the entire movie so that the surprise ending is fitting though unexpected and the audience accepts it. A memorable example is from the horror film *Carrie* (1976). As Carrie's worst bully lays flowers on her headstone, Carrie reaches out from the grave and grabs her hand, giving the audience a last fright and Carrie the last strike.

The surprise ending, whether for a film or TV show, should not *jump the shark*,[28] that is, it should not move so far off its premise that it loses its credibility along with viewers. Cognitive scientists have studied plot-twist endings to better understand how the human brain works. A cognitive science professor at Case Western University, Vera Tobin, believes that while we don't like being misled in real life, we accept it and actually enjoy it in movies and TV shows because the twist endings have been properly set up:

> I think in a lot of circumstances, people tend to think of plot twists as being in some way opposed to—you know, they're gimmicky. They're operating on a level that is counter to these other sorts of literary and filmic values of immersive storytelling, vivid characterization, depth, and complexity and so on. But actually, often, they capitalize on exactly those things. . . . So what a story can do for you is construct this insight experience, where you feel not that something has blindsided you or that you were just taken

27. Shankar Vedantam, Laura Kwerel, and Tara Boyle, "Why We Love Surprises: The Psychology of Plot Twists," *Hidden Brain: A Conversation about Life's Unseen Patterns*, NPR, December 23, 2019, https://www.npr.org /series/423302056/hidden-brain.

28. Coined in 1985 from a 1977 episode of *Happy Days* in which the Fonz waterskied over a shark.

by surprise, but this experience feels as if you have a real "aha moment" about how things fit together. And that is something that humans like a lot.[29]

Sometimes people do not appreciate surprises because they feel misled or manipulated.

We all edit our words about our life and experiences. Documentary filmmakers and news crews choose what angles to capture—they cannot and do not represent 360 degrees of an event. Film editors routinely string words together to show points of view or create performances. Spielberg's editor Michael Kahn (*Jurassic Park, Schindler's List, West Side Story*) acknowledges this: "Editing is manipulation whether it's for a laugh, a sigh, or a fright."[30] When the stringing together misrepresents what a person said—not uncommon on reality shows—it is known as a *Frankenbite*. While there is no Hippocratic oath of filmmaking, the editor has most certainly crossed an ethical line and created a monster of reality. Preachers, too, edit words and make interpretive choices, which some might experience as manipulative.

The gospel itself is the twist that surprises. However, we've become so used to it that we need more. Most of us hearing the story of Jesus in the Gospels have heard it before. We can't even remember our first hearing. Because it's so rare that anyone who hasn't heard the story is actually in church, preachers have to take that old, old story and make it new, new.

In the final move of a sermon on the parable in Matthew 22:1–14, a preacher explicitly names that the parable offers a twist.[31]

> Imagine this with me for a moment.
> Jesus sets up this parable format with the first section.
> He says,
>> "Here is a situation you know, intimately, because you've lived it.
>> A king honoring some above others.
>> A king who dismisses and rejects those who displease him.
>>> "Now, a twist: Here he welcomes all, without exception."
>
> Then, the second section comes along:
>> "Here is another situation you know,

29. Vedantam, Kwerel, and Boyle, "Why We Love Surprises."

30. From the documentary *The Cutting Edge: The Magic of Movie Editing*, directed by Wendy Apple, written by Mark Jonathan Harris (Burbank, CA: Warner Home Video, 2004), DVD.

31. Shared by permission of Emily DeMarco.

the king acting just like the king we knew from the beginning of
   the last story.
Excluding people,
exiling people,
inflicting harm on the community."

And now we can imagine that Jesus,
   who, remember, is teaching us about the kingdom of heaven,
      the world as God intends it to be,
   stops there, Pauses [pause]

And then looks at us as if to say: Now you tell me the twist.

Jesus is inviting us,
   All of us, without exception
To step into this story,
And change the note that it ends on.

We're asked, What is the missing good news,
   and how can we proclaim it for those in need? . . .

Jesus has finished His teaching for today,
   and He looks at us,
   and He reminds us:

   You don't need to be afraid of what comes next.
   You don't need to be afraid to be found wanting.
   You are free to go be the twist in the story.

The preacher wisely knows that the gospel itself is no longer enough of
a twist. The twist the preacher offers is that the parable is unfinished.
The ending is open, and it is up to us to write it, to live it, to be the
inbreaking of God into the world. That is the twist of the twist.

Circular Ending

Many films have circular endings: the opening and closing scenes that
bookend the show occur in the same location, sometimes with similar or
even identical shots, words, or character actions. Circular endings constitute a homecoming of sorts and leave viewers content as the story winds
up at its starting point. Examples include *The Wizard of Oz* (1939), with
Dorothy returning to Kansas from Oz, intoning, "There's no place like

home," and *1917* (2019), which begins with a soldier sleeping against a tree being roused into a battle mission and ends with him leaning against a tree the next day, fatigued and traumatized.

Another type of circular ending occurs when the main character returns to a significant place in their past, usually their childhood home. A couple of examples are the Oscar-winning drama *The Trip to Bountiful* (1985), which followed an elderly Texan's journey to the remnants of her childhood farmhouse, and the TV comedy series *Newhart* (1982–90), which centered on Newhart's character, innkeeper-author Dick Loudon, and concluded by circling back to Newhart's earlier series, *The Bob Newhart Show* (1972–78), having him wake up as psychologist Robert Hartley in bed with his 1970s wife, realizing he'd dreamed the entire second series.

Circular endings, like other kinds of endings, often instigate new beginnings with an action: a wedding to a new spouse, a child born, a person emigrating, or an artist able to create again. Pastor and homiletician David Lose has commented on this bookending technique:

One of the questions preachers often ask is whether the sermon closing should relate directly to the sermon opening. Most of us aspire to that because we sense the aesthetic pleasure of the bookending of a sermon with an opening and a closing. But I don't think we need to feel that kind of pressure each and every week. One way to gauge how closely your sermon closing ought to relate to its opening is to simply ask yourself how powerful of an opening it was. The more powerful the sermon opening, the more demand there is for the preacher to return to that theme or that question or that story in the closing. If on the other hand the sermon opening really is serving to get the sermon moving, then the sermon closing is free to move in whatever direction you want.[32]

Symbolism, Image, Dialogue

The filmmaker has likely already infused *symbolism* into a film in order for it to be effective in the ending, but we'll discuss it here since this

32. David Lose, "Closing the Sermon," audio lecture, Center for Biblical Preaching, Luther Seminary, St. Paul, MN, January 2008, https://www.luthersem.edu/story/2007/05/21/center-for-biblical-preaching-offers-wealth-of-resources.

is where any symbolism reaches final fruition or resolution. Filmmakers inject films with four major types of symbolism: objects, setting, character, and color. The circular ending of *Citizen Kane* (1941) rests on an object. The ending recalls Kane's dying word, "Rosebud," uttered at the film's beginning, and reveals that Rosebud is a sled, embodying his lost childhood. *Selma* (2014) ends with the bloody 1965 march completed and the Rev. Martin Luther King Jr. giving his "How Long, Not Long" speech on the steps of the capitol building in Montgomery, Alabama. The speech and the movie conclude with King exhorting, "His truth is marching on" and "Glory, Hallelujah," symbolic of the long road ahead for civil rights.

All shows have color palettes that directors devise with the aid of the set designer, wardrobe supervisor, and cinematographer. Often the colors are selected to have symbolic meaning, although red (or any other color) for one director in one movie can mean something entirely different from red in another movie by another director. In *Schindler's List* (1993), Spielberg's palette ranged from one end of the gray scale to the other as he saw life lived in concentration camps in "lifeless light."[33] There were two exceptions to his black-and-white filming: the red coat of a little Jewish girl who personifies the one million children murdered in the Holocaust, and the ending. At the end of the film in black-and-white, we see a line of liberated people exiting Schindler's factory, having been saved by him. This line turns to color and becomes modern-day, living "Schindler Jews," as the subtitle states. They and their descendants each pass by Schindler's grave and put a stone on it. Spielberg said the living color and people in "that ending was a way to verify that everything in the movie was true."[34]

The following sermon offers an example of both bookending the sermon opening and closing as well as using a powerful and memorable symbol. Episcopal Bishop Michael Curry utilized these techniques in his sermon preached at the wedding of Prince Harry and Meghan

---

33. Ros Tibbs, "Spielberg Explains the Powerful Ending of 'Schindler's List," *Far Out,* February 1, 2023, https://faroutmagazine.co.uk/steven-spielberg -explains-ending-schindlers-list/.

34. Zac Ntim, "Steven Spielberg on Ending 'Schindler's List' with Cemetery Scene," Deadline, January 29, 2023, https://deadline.com/2023/01/steven-spielberg -schindlers-list-cemetery-scene-ending.

Markle that was televised around the world on May 19, 2018.[35] Bishop Curry begins his sermon with a quote from the late Rev. Dr. Martin Luther King Jr.:

> We must discover the power of love, the redemptive power of love. And when we do that, we will make of this old world a new world, for love is the only way.

Bishop Curry then reflects on the quote:

> There's power in love. Don't underestimate it. Don't even over-sentimentalize it. There's power, power in love.

The opening, in terms offered by Lose, has quite an emotional impact and therefore begs to be returned to at some point in the sermon. For now, let's jump to the time in the sermon when Bishop Curry signals that he is moving toward his closing. He says so explicitly as he addresses the couple directly, "Pierre Teilhard de Chardin—and with this I will sit down, we gotta get you all married." After offering some background on the French Jesuit priest, Curry highlights the importance of fire in both his scientific and theological writings.

> The discovery, or invention, or harnessing of fire was one of the great scientific and technological discoveries in all of human history.
>
> Fire to a great extent made human civilization possible.
>
> Fire made it possible to cook food and to provide sanitary ways of eating which reduced the spread of disease in its time.
> Fire made it possible to heat warm environments and thereby made human migration around the world a possibility, even into colder climates.
> Fire made it possible—there was no Bronze Age without fire,
> no Iron Age without fire,
> no Industrial Revolution without fire.
> The advances of fire and technology are greatly dependent on the human ability and capacity to take fire and use it for human good.

35. Michael Curry, "The Power of Love" (sermon, St. George's Chapel, Windsor Castle, England, May 20, 2018, https://www.npr.org/sections/thetwo-way/2018/05/20/612798691/bishop-michael-currys-royal-wedding-sermon-full-text-of-the-power-of-love.

Then there's a brief interlude addressing how those gathered, including Curry himself, arrived at the wedding—noting that "controlled, harnessed fire" made it possible to drive and fly.

> Fire makes all of that possible, and de Chardin said fire was one of the greatest discoveries in all of human history. And he then went on to say that if humanity ever harnesses the energy of fire again, if humanity ever captures the energy of love—it will be the second time in history that we have discovered fire.

Fire becomes the driving symbol at the close of this wedding sermon before Curry closes where he began.

> Dr. King was right: we must discover love—the redemptive power of love. And when we do that, we will make of this old world, a new world.

Something has changed since the opening quote in the beginning of the sermon. Curry himself assents to King's proposition, thereby encouraging others to do the same. With that, Curry offers direct communication both to the couple and then to the whole congregation.

> [to the couple] My brother, my sister,
> 　　　　God love you.
> 　　　　God bless you.
> [to the congregation] And may God hold us all in those almighty
> 　　　　hands of love.

Whereas grace serves as a key theme in the closing of Obama's eulogy, fire is the primary symbol in Curry's sermon. Both memorable symbols assist hearers' memory of the sermons. While hearers may not remember exactly what was said about each, they will likely recall the symbol, which might help them to remember the feeling and the charge.

In addition to closing with a symbol, closing with a memorable image is another good option. Just as the opening image of a film is important and makes a first impression, so is a closing image as it contributes a last—and perhaps lasting—image. The decision as to where to leave a story is as important as where to open it. With the opening image, filmmakers seek to engage the audience with the story and characters. Whether the closing image is scary, soothing, revelatory, enigmatic, or something else, it should pack an emotional punch. What will the audience take from the movie when it's over? Something has changed since the opening, and the closing image seals it. The TV series *M*A*S*H* signed off in 1983 with the reverse image of the series opening credits. The opening credits each week portrayed helicopters headed toward a Mobile Army Surgical Hospital in Korea during the war. In the show's finale, the war ends. A helicopter takes off and leaves the hospital camp carrying Hawkeye, the main character. Hawkeye looks down and sees that his buddy BJ on the ground has spelled out "GOODBYE" with rocks—the final image. In the Matthew 3 sermon above, the final memorable image is the preacher herself standing before the congregation as a beloved child of God witnessing to God's grace through a community of supporters.

Finally, along with a memorable image, many movies go out with an ending line that serves the film's story and characters and secures a place in the culture by being widely quoted. *Apocalypse Now* (1979) concludes with Marlon Brando's character, having overstayed in the Vietnamese jungle and lost his moral compass, muttering, "The horror, the horror." At the end of *Back to the Future* (1985), Dr. Emmett Brown tells Marty McFly, "Roads? Where we're going, we don't need roads!" President Ronald Reagan used the line in his 1986 State of the Union address. The last line of Martin Luther King Jr.'s "I Have a Dream" speech serves as a good sermonic example: "Free at last. Free at last. Thank God almighty, we are free at last." Chances are you were able to finish that line, even before you read the last words.

Choosing and Enacting an Ending

Many films have been changed during editing following test screenings. For instance, the original finale of *Fatal Attraction* (1987) had Glenn Close's character, Alex Forrest, committing suicide to frame Dan Gallagher (Michael Douglas) as a vengeful tactic following their affair. After negative reactions from test screenings, a new outcome was filmed: Dan's wife shoots her dead. Although Close was incredibly upset with the new ending, she later admitted that she didn't "think it would become the phenomenon it became if they hadn't changed the ending."[36] Film writer–podcaster Barry Estelhomme says, "The most

36. "Glenn Close, Full Address and Q&A, Oxford Union," May 4, 2018, YouTube video, 44:40, https://www.youtube.com/watch?v=qDWDhntzc-w&t=2815s.

important part of every movie is the last half hour. The way the audience feels about the ending of a film can make or break that movie. . . . One tweak to a movie's ending can turn a great film into a classic." [37] Revising the ending is very important.

It takes trying on for size various endings, one iteration after another, then, in some cases, running it by others to see if it works. How have you changed a sermon ending for the better? How did you know it was better? Again, it's worth noting—keeping track of even—what you do and why in your endings, and how you've revised them for the better. Other than actually preaching the ending to a willing listener or ten, one of the best ways to test it is to practice it out loud.

A sermon ending as written can be a blockbuster. But if you don't deliver it with fitting energy, it won't achieve your desired impact. Above all, know it cold. Do not read it from the page, not any part of it! Be present. Your hearers need to know that they are more important to you than what you have written on the script. Otherwise, it's as if before Dorothy gets back to Kansas, the house lights come on and someone from the local theater walks out to narrate the last page of the script. The result? A powerful ending rendered lifeless. Holbert and McKenzie believe that preachers need to ask themselves,

> What is the most fitting way to end the sermon? Do I want to summarize its teaching, tell a story, complete a story, hold up an image, inspire listeners' emotions with eloquent, poetic language, suggest a specific line of action, invite listeners into a scene either biblical or contemporary, tie up loose ends, or challenge hearers with a question? Whatever choice I make, I need to make sure I have rehearsed my ending carefully, and that I have chosen my words carefully, and that I haven't chosen too many words. [38]

What looks good to the eye on the page may not resound when spoken for the ear. Rehearse until you've got the most natural way of proclaiming the close of your sermon.

37. Barry Estelhomme, "From 'Titanic' to 'Get Out': 10 Movies That Were Made Better by Changing the Ending," Collider, December 9, 2022, https://collider.com/movies-made-better-by-new-ending/#39-army-of-darkness-39-1992.

38. John C. Holbert and Alyce M. McKenzie, *What Not to Say: Avoiding the Common Mistakes That Can Sink Your Sermon* (Louisville, KY: Westminster John Knox Press, 2011), 119.

A Word about "AMEN"

When "The End" pops up on the screen or the credits begin to roll, as is customary today, and the lights come up, moviegoers may become temporarily disoriented as they are dragged back into the chairs and aisles of the theater—the real world. The time it takes to reorient might just be a sign that the ending has done its job. Preachers, do you give your hearers time after you've preached? If something has indeed changed—a knowing about Jesus, a feeling of being fully accepted, a motivation to care for the neighbor—your hearers might need a moment to absorb the impact, to linger in the change they've experienced. The time it takes to reorient might just be a sign that the sermon closing has done its job.

While "The End" may be the quintessential filmic last line (with Porky Pig's announcement, "That's all folks," being a close second), the sermon's "amen" signals "that's a wrap." But since a preacher wants to signal not an end but a new beginning, is amen the best way to end a sermon? In light of the gift that is aesthetic distance, noted above, consider that this word belongs in the mouths of the hearers and not the preacher.

The Hebrew root of the word "amen" (spelled *aleph mem nun,* אמן) appears more than two hundred times in the Bible and means "constant, faithful presence." The root is also foundational to the Hebrew word *em* (אם), which means "mother."[39] Think of the constant presence it takes to care for a young child. This faithfulness/presence/being with has turned into the liturgical call "amen," signifying, "Yes, I'm with it. I am with you." Thus "amen" is not to be demanded or forced; it is an utterance that belongs to the hearer in response to what the preacher has offered, even if asked by the preacher, "Can I get an amen?" Of course, we hope they will offer it. We hope they will be with us.

That's a wrap . . . or is it? Stay tuned.

7

Outtakes

In the days of cutting on film, editors routinely removed edited scenes and sections that had been dropped from the story. These *lifts*—rolled-up pieces of spliced film—were placed in labeled boxes and shelved, ready to be dropped back in if necessary. *Outtakes*—takes not used in editing—were filed similarly. Analogously, writers of all stripes regularly stow ideas in a drawer—more likely a designated folder on their computer today. This chapter is about putting lifts, outtakes, and ideas from previous chapters of this book back into play. We are reviving our darlings and finding them a home here for your consideration.

TRAILERS AND MOVIE POSTERS

> They give away too much of the movie. They're better than the films. They only show the spectacular parts. All the best jokes are in the trailer. They lie. They're the best part of going to the movies. They're too loud.
> —Lisa Kernan, *Coming Attractions: Reading Movie Trailers*

Now that you have incorporated the wisdom of filmmaking into your preaching practices with the hope that it will have the greatest impact on others, there is the challenge of getting a hearing. The film industry has trailers and movie posters to persuade viewers to buy a ticket at the cinema or click Play on their remote. Let's first consider the movie trailer.

A trailer is a mini movie that aims to tell and sell the story of a story in ninety seconds or fewer. Filmmakers invariably divorce themselves from the show's order of scenes in editing a trailer. Anything can go in or out of a trailer—music, VFX, VO, graphics, visuals. Viewers use trailers to reject a movie and save themselves time and money or dismiss them as crass commercials and don't worry about entering a theater in the middle of them. On the other hand, the Independent Film Channel says that "trailers provide a version of cinema that's essentially utopian, in which every film is perfect, if only for two and a half minutes."[1]

Preachers, what would you include (and deliberately not include) in your two-and-a-half-minute trailer for your next sermon? In contemplating a trailer, it is best, once again, to think about your audience. What do they need to see, hear, or know about your upcoming sermon or series of sermons? Think of it as the digital equivalent of that big sign on the front of the church property compelling passersbys to slow down and read the quip. Entice others to "come and see" through your digital trailer sent via YouTube or Facebook. In this era of social media, chances are people might actually give it a thumbs-up, forward, or retweet.

You might also consider using the services of a parishioner to create a *one sheet*, a movie poster, to go along with the trailer. What is the primary image presented? Will it be a person? A community of people? The Trinity? Will you feature an image or a symbol? What words will appear? What colors will you use, and why?

SERIES ARC

Just as movies have character arcs and a beginning, middle, and end, so do TV series and movie sequels, depending on the type of series. The first type, the ongoing series, builds from episode to episode, following a main character or multiple characters and demanding to be viewed in order. *General Hospital* (1963–) and all soap operas constitute ongoing series, as does the *Harry Potter* movie series (2001–11). Each TV season and movie sequel carries the action and surviving characters forward. Each season or sequel contains a beginning, middle, and end and a central question that pings the central question for the entire series.

---

1. Gael Chandler, *Editing for Directors: A Guide for Creative Collaboration* (Studio City, CA: Michael Wiese Productions, 2021), 229–30.

Some conflicts are resolved and others not, priming viewers for the next season or sequel.

The second type of series, the stand-alone series, can be viewed in any order because the episodes don't build on each other—each stands alone. Many comedy series and detective series are stand-alones, including *The Simpsons* (1989–) and *Law and Order* (1990–). Main characters may appear weekly, as in these two series, or each episode in a stand-alone series may have entirely new characters, settings, plots, and even genres. Witness the classic *Twilight Zone* (1958–) series and the British series *Inside No. 9* (2014–) in which the only link between episodes is the number nine seen in an establishing shot, typically in an address. While characters don't develop much over time, because stand-alone series resolve their dilemmas and tie up plotlines with each episode, viewers can sleep easy and won't be tempted to binge-watch . . . or will they? Stand-alone series, like ongoing series, beget *prequels*, spin-offs, and the occasional multipart episodes.

Another example of a stand-alone series is sports shows. A *New York Times* article heralded *Sunday Night Football*'s niche in the TV sphere:

> Prestige dramas and comedies are, in essence, serialized movies, but a football telecast belongs to a different category. It is an extravagant exercise in visual storytelling: an hours-long motion-picture collage, assembled on the fly, pumped up with interstitial music, graffitied with graphics, embellished with hokey human-interest segments and narrated, with varying degrees of wit and magniloquence, by the featured soloists in the broadcast booth. As a technical feat, it's a mindblower: a collective improvisation by a team of hundreds, pulled off with top craftsmanship under conditions of extreme pressure.[2]

The "series" is no stranger to preachers. Preachers are mindful of season, albeit Advent, Christmas, Epiphany, instead of season 1, season 2, season 3. We even have Lent 1, Lent 2, Lent 3, and they are not presented all at once for viewers to binge-watch but are released weekly, on Sunday morning. Preachers can learn practices from filmmakers that keep viewers coming back for more.

---

2. Jody Rosen, "Sunday Night Lights: How America's Most Spectacular TV Show Gets Made," *New York Times Magazine,* December 2, 2023, https://www.nytimes.com/2023/12/02/magazine/sunday-night-football.html.

Sometimes the sermon will function like a stand-alone series with each episode containing a beginning, middle, and end on its own, resolving all conflicts and not introducing new plotlines or characters. In this case, each episode (sermon) can be experienced on its own. Perhaps chapter 6 helped you realize that your sermon closings tend to be open—that is, they end with a question mark or an ellipsis, prompting hearers to fill in the rest of the story—and yet you've been treating each sermon as a stand-alone event. This combination may yield a disconnect—not at insurmountable one, but one that invites you to utilize the best practices of filmmaking to intentionally build on previous weeks and propel us forward. The scriptural texts identified in the lectionary can be useful since they purposefully build on one another as the church moves through a liturgical season.

With an ongoing sermon series, preachers might map out or storyboard the episodes in a season, paying attention to major themes, the big questions, problems to be addressed, characters to be introduced and developed. You might just find yourself developing an intentional multipart series with an eye toward a sequel. Along the way, don't forget to consider the prequel (who was Paul before he became a follower of Jesus?) or spin-off (whatever happened to those women who found the tomb empty?).

CARDING/MAPPING

Many screenwriters use a process called "carding" to organize (and reorganize) their screenplays. This process assists with arranging important elements as well as cutting things that do not belong. The name "carding" refers to the index cards (or sometimes sticky notes) on which the writer writes a brief word or phrase identifying a scene, sequence, or description.

The cards are laid out on a table or tacked onto a wall to produce a big picture of the flow of the show. Cards are shifted around and reordered to "help envision changes, functioning as a moveable storyboard."[3] Carding allows the screenwriter to consider and arrange countless variations until

3. See Meg LeFauve and Lorien McKenna, "Michael Arndt's Act 1 Masterclass (Rebroadcast)," episode 165 of *The Screenwriting Life with Meg LeFauve and Lorien McKenna* (podcast), 5:50, November 16, 2023, https://podcasts.apple.com /us/podcast/the-screenwriting-life-with-meg-lefauve-and-lorien-mckenna /id1501641442?i=1000635043781.

"it feels right." Hollywood screenwriter John August says the purpose is to "work as an editor, trying to find the best flow of scenes and sequences for pacing purposes and story structure building." He adds,

> Pacing is a vital part of the screenwriting process, and index cards serve as an amazing tool to showcase the pacing of your script. . . . When you feature an action sequence within an index card, you're calling attention to a part of the script that is elevated. If you have too few within your action script, you'll see the problem quickly. If you have too many action sequences, they'll stick out like a sore thumb. . . . It's all about balance—and using color cards for certain elements is key to maintaining a visual sense of the balance between action and dramatic scenes and sequences.[4]

For a helpful tutorial on how a screenwriter uses carding, see Academy Original's short video featuring Dustin Lance Black of *Milk* (2008) and *Rustin* (2023).[5]

We encourage preachers to adopt a similar process of mapping sermons for three reasons. First, attending to the organization of content and the progression of major moves, with special attention to the transitions between major moves, will improve your hearers' experience. Second, having fewer words on the page often removes the temptation to just read what's on the page (again, simply reading is not preaching). Third, carding is also useful in editing and rewriting.

To get started mapping, consider the two required pieces of information for a navigation app: a starting point and a destination. At some point in the sermon preparation process, preachers begin to sense such a starting point and a destination. The starting point in preaching is the context, including the occasion. The ending point is where the sermon is headed; that is, what you hope will happen to the hearer (think: function statement). More concretely, the starting point is the opening move and the ending point is the closing move (with the outlier starting point and ending points of context and the function). Preachers then begin to fill in the major components or moves of the sermon. One might be able to identify the elements that are included but not

4. Ken Miyamoto, "Hollywood Screenwriter John August's 10 Best Index Card Practices," Screencraft, December 30, 2019, https://screencraft.org/blog/hollywood-screenwriter-john-augusts-10-best-index-card-practices/.

5. "Creative Spark: Dustin Lance Black," Academy Originals, May 26, 2014, YouTube video, 6:56, https://www.youtube.com/watch?v=vrvawtrRxsw.

perhaps the best order to arrange them. That's the time to start mapping the sermon, keeping in mind that everything remains movable.

Mapping is more helpful than outlining because it's active; it adds components like distance and time and pacing and turns. Some major moves are twenty miles long, so to speak; others are a mere five miles, and others still are akin to quick roundabouts. Notice detours that might frustrate hearers. Mapping helps preachers recognize that in order to take them from San Francisco to Phoenix, you likely need not make a stop in Nashville. Sometimes preachers will take the fastest route, and other times they'll choose the shortest distance. While efficiency is not always the goal, it is worth reconsidering the longer route or a detour lest those in the car start asking, "How many more miles?" or complaining, "I'm feeling carsick." And remember that you have to slow down, way down, for curvy roads or sharp corners (think: prophetic preaching).

Just as screenwriters often color-code their cards for emotion or to differentiate between, for example, an action scene and a dialogue scene, preachers might use one color every time they refer to the first century, a different color when speaking in the present, and a third color for transitions. Seeing the big picture of those colors on the board in the writer's room (or on the computer screen) can be illuminating.

The goal is to have enough on the map to jog one's memory while preaching and not to include so many words that one is tempted to simply read. Rehearsing from the map is like a singer practicing her aria over and over in preparation for a recital. With each practice, you might find yourself rearranging cards, shortening moves, or adjusting transitional phrases. The result is a meaningful delivery that the hearers can follow, perhaps even losing track of time as they enjoy the ride.

There is no set way to develop the sermon map. Here's how one preacher describes her process in a reflection paper for a preaching class:

> I developed my map by first creating a rough transcript for the sermon. After that was complete, I separated the major moves with page breaks and then used those to develop the map. When creating the map itself, I first used Post-it Notes with a word or two to see where things would go. Then I utilized PowerPoint to recreate the Post-it map, but with more content filled in. While editing the map to make it most useful, I had to practice and

practice and practice. First, I practiced with the script in front of me, so that I could get the words into my bones. After that I moved on to the sermon map. While practicing with the sermon map, I would make a note of where I would get tripped up to see if I should add a prompt to the map.[6]

Perhaps you will have an experience similar to the following reflections by novice preachers when they tried their hand at sermon-mapping (albeit self-consciously at first):

— By visualizing the sermon in the map format, I could identify areas where transitions could be strengthened or changed, enhancing the overall flow of the message and assisting me in maintaining clarity and focus for the delivery.[7]
— The main benefit of developing a sermon map was that it increased my familiarity with the content. In putting together and then editing the map, I was really internalizing each major move. Distilling the moves down into major themes and phrases crystallized them for me so I remained focused throughout my preaching. This also led to a second benefit: I was able to make eye contact with the congregation much more frequently. I [could see] the nods of affirmation.[8]
— Preaching from the map was both nerve-wracking and freeing. While I had some anxiety about losing my place or not remembering to project my voice because I was so concerned with remembering my words, the benefits of being able to engage more fully with the congregation were huge. I was more attentive to those in front of me and God with me, which was exactly what the sermon was all about. Developing the sermon map had numerous benefits, but the primary one was how much more engaged I was with the congregation while preaching because I had the sermon already in my bones. This allowed me to be more flexible in the moment and vary my pacing and tone throughout the sermon as well.[9]

6. Used by permission of Sarah Jessop Street.
7. Used by permission of Brenda Lussier.
8. Used by permission of Emily DeMarco.
9. Used by permission of Sarah Jessop Street.

EDITING ON THE FLY

Some shows do not have the luxury of spending months in the editing room to perfect them as feature films do. Televised live performances and sports events are edited live "on the fly." Rob Hyland, coordinating producer of *Sunday Night Football* (SNF), explains,

> Every play can take you in a different direction. You can go to a replay to help support what your announcers are talking about. You can show America a different angle on a play. Or you can take America in a whole new direction narratively. You can go to a preproduced element to showcase something interesting about a specific athlete or coach. You can go to a graphic to help support a story line or to introduce a new story line.[10]

To make this editing on the fly possible, meticulous preproduction planning is necessary. For SNF, preproduction includes the setup of multiple cameras, microphones, a 144-channel sound-mixing console, and a live switcher to cut between all the elements (players, announcers, crowd, scoreboard, replays, graphic clips of stats, and so on) along with preediting video clips about players and coaches and a run-through of the facility.

> Directing a football game is both diabolically complex and simple in its essence. You must have command of vast amounts of information and comfort with state-of-the-art machines. You have to know where each camera is positioned and how to locate its feed amid the dizzying grid of monitors. Every week, you have to commit to memory the names and uniform numbers of dozens of players. You must be capable of conducting simultaneous conversations with the dozens of camera operators hooked into your headset and with your colleagues in the truck, while listening closely to the live audio going out on air. And you need to do all this while calling out a virtually nonstop series of commands to the technical director on your right. Yet the heart of the gig is straightforward. "It's storytelling," [director Drew] Esocoff says.[11]

10. Rosen, "Sunday Night Lights."
11. Rosen, "Sunday Night Lights."

The kind of preproduction work that goes into live sports storytelling is not unlike the work required to put together an entire worship service, including the sermon. In order to make possible editing the liturgy or sermon on the fly, meticulous preproduction planning is necessary. As a preacher who tried the meticulous preplanning of working with a sermon map said, getting the sermon "in my bones . . . allowed me to be more flexible in the moment and vary my pacing and tone throughout the sermon as well." For every preacher who has received the news of a death of a congregation member or an emergency in the community at the start of worship, knowing the sermon in one's bones is key in order to edit on the fly.

SOUNDTRACK

> The final anchoring point of the movie soundtrack is the music. Music provides an emotional bedrock for a film.
> —Skywalker Sound Ltd.

Not much has been said in these pages about film scores, but it's not lost on us that some preaching has the added element of the organist backing up the preacher with what is essentially a musical score. The time signature and the key signature create meaning. The pauses and rests are just as impactful as the notes.

We've all come to expect realistic, natural sound in movies. In truth, sound in films is anything but realistic or natural: a dozen sound editors and mixers have created and positioned the audio so that the audience will accept the world of the movie. We accept that Barcelona sounds like this, the Wild West sounded like that, and Middle Earth sounds like it does due to the world of sound conceived by the sound team: sound designer, sound editors, and sound mixers.

The music team—composer and music editor—also strongly influences how the audience feels about a show's subject, characters, themes, and plot. Music anticipates and foreshadows action, for instance, by warning that evil is just around the corner. John Williams's violin-driven score in *Schindler's List* (1993), played by Itzhak Perlman, hauntingly mirrors the tragedy of the Holocaust. Music can counter what's on the screen to convey a larger truth or offset the violence unfolding. It can also conjure a time or a place. The pop tunes of the 1950s and 1960s in

The Marvelous Mrs. Maisel (2017–23) helped aurally plant the series in mid-century New York City.

Whether the filmmaker is taking viewers down a rabbit hole or inside a computer, to outer space or to the past, sound and music play a vital role in placing them in that world and making them accept the creatures—hobbits, robots, or humans—that inhabit it. And that role includes the sound of silence. Sound design invariably contains planned sections of silence or minimal sound. (No show is entirely silent, as there is always ambient sound. If the filmmaker drops out all sound, they risk hostile glares at the projection booth and channel surfing.) Silence, especially following a gripping scene or a cacophony of sounds, lets the audience take a breath and recover.

Well-designed and mixed sound and music voice a movie's visuals and can set the pace for a scene, signal changes in time or place, heighten the action or diminish it, and smooth scene transitions. They can also connect characters, images, locations, and ideas. Filmmakers also use sound and music to define characters—both animated and human—by building their aural persona, so viewers can know what they're feeling and experiencing.

In chapter 4, we discussed how filmmakers often cut in beats, changes of action within a scene. Thinking in beats is also useful to sound and music designers in conceiving how a scene should sound, what sounds and music should be used, and where they should come in. A beat can call for a change in tempo, pitch, volume, or intensity of music or effects. Beats can also help determine where to punch up a word or dial it down to a murmur, and when to plaster the picture with sound effects or restrict audio to a single, recurring effect or silence (ambience). Sound and music sustain and are an integral part of a film's voice and vision. Music is the emotional bedrock of a film, cueing how we feel about characters and how much we feel.

Preachers, even if you are not backed up by an organist, it is worth considering how you might score your sermon musically. Mark up your script with staccatos, crescendos, decrescendos, and rests. Identify where it's in a minor key and why. Where does the key signature change, and how do you indicate that? Which instruments best represent Jesus's voice? What sound effects might depict the tearing of the heavens? What does that Roman soldier's spade sound like when it hits the stone floor of the echoey chamber in Pilate's praetorium? Invite others, especially members of your church with musical acumen, to describe how they would orchestrate a certain biblical story. While you can, you need not actually compose the piece to get the benefit. The imaginative exercise alone offers insight into how the story is impacting their lives and is much more interesting than simply responding to "What do you think the text means?"

ARTIFICIAL INTELLIGENCE (AI)

Every story needs a villain. For decades, artificial intelligence has been presented as a mysterious, powerful antagonist in Hollywood. HAL (*2001: A Space Odyssey*, 1968), Ava (*Ex-Machina*, 2014), and Ultron (*Avengers: Age of Ultron*, 2015) are all part of a broader narrative that paints AI as the personification of technology's threat to humankind.[12]
—Sunny Dhillon

While the dangers of AI are much discussed, how this developing technology will play out in all aspects of society is a "stay tuned" concern. Here we will spotlight how AI is playing a positive role and being challenged in filmmaking today and look at its homiletical implications.

— In 1914, a camera operator using a hand crank filmed a conversation between William "Buffalo Bill" Cody and Oglala Lakota leader Siŋté Máza in Plains Indian Sign Language. The footage, shot at nineteen frames per second (fps),[13] showed unnatural, jerky human motion as well as poor-quality frames. Digital artist Matt Loughrey created an AI algorithm to generate new frames and speed up the frame rate to 60 fps so that the men's actions looked natural and are in real time. "You can see Cody's pocket watch moving. You can see his hair moving," Loughrey said.[14]
— In 2016, Twentieth Century Fox released *Morgan,* a sci-fi horror film about an artificially engineered human named Morgan, and created the trailer using AI.
— In mid-2023, the Writers Guild of America (WGA) and Screen Actors Guild–American Federation of Television and Radio Artists

12. Sunny Dhillon, "How AI Will Augment Human Creativity in Film Production," *Variety,* July 20, 2023.

13. Modern rates are twenty-four fps for film and sixty fps for high-definition (HD) digital video.

14. Mindy Weisberger, "Artificial Intelligence Lends New Life to Old Films," Live Science, June 23, 2020, https://www.livescience.com/19th-century-films -restored.html.

(SAG-AFTRA) went on strike against the studios, AI being a major point of contention.

Hollywood filmmakers are beginning to employ AI in mundane tasks that revolve around gathering, tracking, and analyzing data to save time and money. These tasks include preproduction planning and audience analysis to predict box office intake. AI is also finding uses in postproduction, such as the generation of transcripts, the creation of CGI, and VFX tasks like the removal of unwanted objects from the frame, such as boom mics, wires (that helped actors "fly"), and anachronistic items in period pieces. In short, AI is performing droid work, as the two following examples show.

To create the trailer for *Morgan,* Twentieth Century Fox called on IBM, which in turn called on Watson, its AI software. GeekWire's Alan Boyle reported, "First, the Watson research team had the software analyze 100 trailers from other horror movies. The AI used statistical methods to tag scenes within each trailer, drawing upon labels from a list of 24 emotions and 22,000 scene categories. The software also analyzed the musical score, character voices and scene composition, rating them on a scariness scale."[15] After the team loaded the final sound-mixed cut of *Morgan* into the computer, "Watson selected the top 10 scenes for a horror-movie trailer, and then it was up to a human filmmaker at IBM to put together those scenes in a dramatic way and add a soundtrack. . . . The entire process took about 24 hours, compared to the typical 10- to 30-day process for creating a movie trailer."[16]

AI has landed a continuing role in film archiving and restoration to remaster old movies by filling in and reconstructing missing and damaged frames. Matt Loughrey used the algorithm he created to restore the 1914 Buffalo Bill and Siŋté Máza clip to upgrade other vintage film clips and stills to HD quality. He ruminates on a clip of street traffic in New York City in 1896 that he restored, which was shot at sixteen fps: "It's like some version of time travel. There's all these little stories going on that you just wouldn't catch at 16 fps."[17]

Homiletically speaking, there is much to be nervous about as AI becomes more accessible. Perhaps of primary concern is a preacher using sermons crafted by AI. Then again, utilizing another's sermon

---

15. Alan Boyle, "Be Afraid. Be Very Afraid: IBM's Watson Makes AI Trailer about 'Morgan' AI Movie," GeekWire, August 31, 2016.

16. Boyle, "Be Afraid."

17. Weisberger, "Artificial Intelligence Lends New Life to Old Films."

has been around for ages. It takes only ten seconds to pilfer an illustration, or even an entire sermon, from the internet. This happens even though we know the power of a sermon crafted with a keen eye toward a community of people in all their particularities for the characteristics of their time and place. Apparently AI is quite good at crafting a cohesive and meaningful sermon as long as one inputs the right elements. It remains to be seen to what extent this will be utilized and, even more, considered faithful. For now, just as the film industry is harnessing AI for some mundane tasks, so, too, might preachers utilize AI to save time and energy. Here are three ideas:

1. Utilize AI as an upgraded search engine to obtain a more well-rounded list of scholarly biblical commentaries and conversation partners. Preachers will need to employ and even increase their critical-reading skills to discern when something not fitting or faithful is proposed.
2. Just as the film industry had Watson conjure a trailer, so, too, might preachers have AI create a trailer by inputting sermon content. This task might also reveal to preachers both missing and unnecessary elements.
3. If you are not artistically inclined and cannot find someone in your midst to put together a "movie" poster for an upcoming sermon, AI might be your go-to creator. For a recent sermon, a student preacher input the verses from a biblical story. The image produced was stunningly apocalyptic. No doubt AI was using a more secular view of religious apocalyptic visions, which offered the student a foil against which he could set a more tolerable and, in his interpretation of Scripture, faithful hidden and revealed God.

TAG

Both movies and TV shows can incorporate an *epilogue,* an integral part of the story that follows its conclusion and gives extra information, often in white text over a black background, about what finally happened to the characters—usually the real people they're based on. A *tag,* however, is strictly a TV construct. A short scene of one to three minutes, a tag follows the end of a TV show, appearing after the final commercial. Frequently it runs next to the end credits in what's termed the "squeeze and tease." A tag resolves a minor plot or shows an aftereffect of the episode. Usually it's a lighthearted, satisfying "button." The antithesis of a teaser, a tag is a bonus scene not integral to the plot that will be the first scene dropped if the show is syndicated. Shows that invariably inserted tags are *The Office, Modern Family,* and *Blackish.* The feature film equivalent would be scenes, gags, bloopers, or outtakes that play during end credits.

Example: The final tag for the final episode of *Blackish* in 2022 is a bookending button. In the series' opening scene, we meet the Johnsons, a Black family who live in a white, upscale neighborhood. Via his VO, we get the father's trajectory: "I guess for a kid from the hood, I'm living the American dream. The only problem is, whatever American had this dream probably wasn't where I'm from." The Johnsons coexist amicably with Janine, a white neighbor who is well-meaning yet ignorant and racist. In the series' last episode, the Johnsons move to a Black neighborhood. In the episode's tag, a Latinx couple move into the Johnsons's former house, remarking, "We are living the American dream." Then Janine stops by, leading with a friendly "Hola."

A tag in the preaching world might not be bloopers or gags. However, preachers can share some of those exegetical discoveries and homiletical insights that didn't make it into the sermon. The postsermon talkback could be a tag. Or consider placing a brief document with "show notes" in the narthex for people to pick up if they're interested. Any of these tags might resolve your hearers' wonderings. Then again, they may spark new ones—and that's a good thing. We want hearers to channel baby Maggie, who ends *The Simpsons Movie* (2007) by asking, "Sequel?" Yes, in fact. Come back next Sunday for more.

We'd close this chapter with "The End" or "That's all folks," but it's really just a beginning. We could say "amen," but it's for you to decide if you're with us.

```
CUT TO:

Over-the-shoulder shot of energetic
preacher in the pulpit addressing an
engrossed congregation.

                              FADE OUT
```

Credits

If a book is a journey, it doesn't reach its final destination without input, information, and encouragement along the way. The authors give thanks to all the creators of all the books, papers, essays, articles, sermons, movies, TV shows, and YouTube videos that informed our thinking (see bibliography). We are ever grateful to Glenda Sharp, hiker extraordinaire, who introduced us. Major credit and thanks go to Wes Allen for championing and astutely editing the book and pioneering the "Preaching and . . ." series. Alyce McKenzie, Director of the Perkins Center for Preaching Excellence, has also been a steadfast supporter, as have David Dobson and his design and editing team, including copyeditor Tina Noll and senior editor Daniel Braden, at Westminster John Knox Press. Other colleagues, friends, and family members who offered enthusiastic support are Suzanne Long, Sherry Green, Bob Herring, Marcia McFee, Kip Pearson, Faye Orton Snyder, Janie Spahr, Jason Wilkinson, participants in the preaching and filmmaking workshops at Princeton Seminary's Engle Institute for Preaching and the 2024 Byberg Preaching Conference in Seaside, Oregon, and students at Pacific Lutheran Theological Seminary in Berkeley, California.

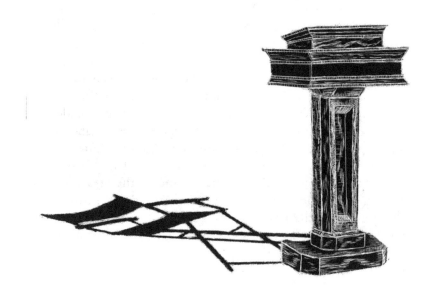

Figure 2 Image courtesy of Suzanne M. Long

Key Filmmaking Terms

action. What takes place in front of the camera after the director says "action" and before they say "cut."

action scene. A scene driven by physical actions (car chase, lovemaking, dance number, etc.) or occurrences (storm, sunset, hurricane, etc.). An action scene can contain significant dialogue and works best when it shows human reactions and motivations. See also **dialogue scene** and **montage scene**.

adapted screenplay. Script based on original work from another medium, such as a play, novel, video game, or toy.

anaphora. Repeating words, phrases, sentences, or images in speeches, poetry, and other writing and films.

angle. How the camera shot shows a subject through framing (wide, medium, close-up, etc.), perspective (overhead, high, low, eye level, etc.), and movement (pan, tilt, track, etc.).

antagonist. The character (or characters, institution, or force) who actively works against the protagonist to stop them from achieving their goal. See also **protagonist**.

anticlimax. A letdown after a climactic moment or an ending that is disappointing or less important, dramatic, or exciting than expected, such as a romance that fizzles after the lead-up to a big kiss.

antihero. Principal character who lacks traditional hero qualities because they live outside society or have challenging dark sides or moral defects: the Joker (*Batman*), Harley Quinn (*Suicide Squad*), Cassie Thomas (*Promising Young Woman*), and Walter White (*Breaking Bad*).

arc. See **character arc**.

archetype. A familiar type of character with recognizable traits, values, and ways of processing information and making decisions, such as the "take no prisoners" leader, the reluctant warrior, the tough parent with a heart of gold.

ASL. Average shot length of an edit in a film.

atmosphere. Elements of a scene or entire film that include weather, sound, time period, setting, mood, and tone, which affect viewers' perceptions and feelings in often not easily definable ways.

auteur theory. The idea, credited to French New Wave filmmakers, that the true author of a film is not the screenwriter but a director with a distinct style, Hitchcock being their prime example.

backstory. Prior events or history that answer questions about a character's actions, reactions, relationships, and motivations, such as why Walter White in *Breaking Bad* starts cooking meth. Backstory is the story before the story that only the screenwriter may know; it may be spooled out via flashbacks, as in *Casablanca* and *Slumdog Millionaire,* or not shown at all.

beat. Plot point or an action where something happens or changes in a scene. Three beats from *The Wizard of Oz* are (1) Dorothy's house lands on the ground, (2) Dorothy emerges to Oz, (3) the Munchkins see her.

beat sheet. Using bullet points, a beat sheet identifies the critical plot points and events in each act of an episodic TV show or a full movie script. A popular story structure device, a beat sheet uses specific beats, such as opening image, introduction, midpoint, low point, climax, resolution, and ending, to outline the script.

Bechdel Test. A method of evaluating the representation of women in movies and fiction. A film passes the test if at least two featured women talk to each other about something other than a man.

blocking. Positioning of actor on set or location; where they will move from and to in relation to the camera, other characters, and objects.

blue sky. To brainstorm ideas as if the sky were the limit. This business term is applied to writers or other creative filmmakers when they freely throw out fresh scenes, characters, plot twists, and so on.

bookend. Related scene or shot that starts and finishes—bookends—a show. The first scene or shot sets up the show and the second, which can be identical, provides the conclusion.

catharsis. An emotional release experienced by the audience, brought about by their living and breathing with a character who stimulates strong, buried emotions, often of loss due to tragedy.

CGI. Computer-generated image.

character arc. The evolution, for better or worse, of a character from their first appearance in the story until their last.

CinemaScope. Also called *scope.* A widescreen format that uses an anamorphic lens to shoot and project images that are nearly two and a half times as wide as they are high.

cinematic. Writing that evokes a film due to its being visual and moving in scenes.

cinematic literacy. Ability to decipher and interpret the content and language of films as told with pictures and sounds via acting, directing, cinematography, and editing.

cinema verité. French term for "truthful cinema." An improvisational, documentary style of filmmaking that eschews narration and actors and employs a minimal crew and equipment to expose hidden truths and subjects.

climax. The highest, most exciting point of a film, always occurring shortly before the end and followed by the resolution of the drama.

closed ending. Conclusion that ties up all the knots, making clear how the story ends, giving closure to all characters, answering all questions, and resolving all conflicts. See also **open ending** and **hybrid ending**.

conflict. Struggle between opposing forces or characters. The struggle may be within a character, between characters, or with nature, God, destiny, change, ethics, morality, society, or technology. Whatever the conflict, it's a vital element in storytelling.

continuity. Maintaining physical relationships, performance, action, and narrative flow of the filmed scene from cut to cut (or, during filming, from shot to shot).

coverage. All nonmaster shots, such as wide, close, and medium shots, overhead shots, inserts, POVs.

crosscut. Two (or more) dependent lines of action—characters, settings, or subjects—that interact directly and are aware of each other. The scenes depend on each other and don't function without being crosscut.

cut. See **shots, takes, edits, and cuts.**

cutaway. Any shot—ordinarily a close-up—that will be used to cut away from the main action in the master shot.

cut point. Also called *edit point.* Place in a shot where editor decides to cut to another shot.

cutter. See **editor.**

dailies. Footage, normally shot the previous day, that arrives daily in the editing room from the production crew.

denouement. The final outcome of a show that follows the climax and concludes, if not resolves, the conflict.

dialogue scene. A scene primarily driven by the words spoken by and between people or characters. A dialogue scene can contain significant action, but the essence of the scene is found in the words. Test: If the scene makes little sense when run silently, it's a dialogue scene. See also **action scene** and **montage scene**.

digital editing system. Computer used to edit digital audio and video input from files, film, or tape.

director. Filmmaker who interacts with producers and supervises talent and crew to achieve the vision of a show from script through production and editing to the final, mixed show. The director has the creative vision and authority on all shows except on television shows, where that role belongs to the executive producer or showrunner (for episodic series).

dissolve. A transitional effect where the first/outgoing shot disappears as the second/incoming shot appears.

documentary. A genre of film that records (documents) modern reality or past events, time periods, civilizations, institutions, lives, and so on as factually as possible to educate or inform viewers.

drama. A genre of narrative fiction that is serious in tone and pits characters against each other, themselves, the environment, the government. Can be parsed into subcategories, such as crime drama, dramedy (comic drama), soap opera, legal drama.

Easter egg. A hidden element in a film, video game, or software deliberately inserted by the creator to amuse astute viewers. It can be an image, inside joke, secret reference, or homage to an earlier film, character, game. The movie *Twister* (1996) centered on a cyclone-chasing couple who deploy a tornado detection device named Dorothy, one of the Easter eggs recalling *The Wizard of Oz*.

edit. See **shots, takes, edits, and cuts.**

editor. Also called *picture editor* or *cutter*. Person who puts the footage together to create the show.

edit point. See **cut point.**

ellipsis. A screenwriter puts "..." (an ellipsis) in a script to tighten the story by omitting sections and shortening time. This translates to the edited footage as a transition between shots or scenes, such as a cut or dissolve.

epilogue. An epilogue follows the conclusion (denouement) of the story and gives extra information, often in white text over a black background, about what finally happened to the characters in real life. See also **denouement.**

epiphany. The "aha!" moment when the protagonist experiences a story-changing realization right before or after a film's climax.

establishing shot. The shot—typically a wide shot or long shot—that encompasses all the action to show the viewer where the scene takes place. Ordinarily placed at the beginning of a scene, it may include the characters or they may be introduced—established—in later shots.

executive producer (EP). Head producer who steers the show to make sure it arrives on time, on budget, and meets delivery requirements. The EP may contribute financially (theatrical films) or be the liaison to the studio or other financial backer(s) (features and TV shows). The EP hires other producers and staff and may be the writer-creator of the project. When a show has more than one EP, the duties will be divided: one EP may oversee the writing and production, another post, and a third be credited in name only and have no EP responsibilities.

exposition. Series of shots or scenes at the beginning of a film that set its time, place, situation, characters, tone, and/or theme. Equivalent to prologue in literature.

extend. Lengthen a scene cut during editing.

fade in. A dissolve to a filmed shot from black, sometimes white, and once in a great while yellow, blue, or another color.

fade out. A dissolve from a filmed shot to black, sometimes white, and once in a great while yellow, blue, or another color.

film noir. Film genre dating from the 1940s characterized by harsh lighting and jaded characters such as private eyes and femmes fatales populating underworld urban settings where the light is low, the tension high, and crimes of passion and greed in the offing. Examples: *Double Indemnity* and *The Maltese Falcon*.

film within a film. Also called *story within a story.* A movie that has a separate movie going on inside, such as Francois Truffaut's *Day for Night.* The main characters may or may not be aware of the film and sometimes even try to jump into it or interact with the film's characters, as in Buster Keaton's *Sherlock Junior* and Woody Allen's *The Purple Rose of Cairo.*

final cut. Also called *locked cut.* Final edited version of the show. Created by the editor and determined by the person in charge of the final cut: director, producer, or client. Once a show is locked, sound editing and mixing take place to complete the release version that viewers will see.

flashback. Shot, sequence of shots, or scene that transports the story into the past. A flashback serves to provide backstory or contextualize an event, relationship, or person's life.

flash cut. A short cut of a few frames that quickly and intensely gets inside a character's mind.

flash-forward. Shot, sequence of shots, or scene that transports the story into the future.

focus group. An audience put together by a studio to watch and give feedback on the impact of a movie or TV pilot before editing is finished, when changes can still be made.

foreshadow. To give a hint of what is to come with dialogue, music, sound effects, or a visual clue, such as an image or symbol. Foreshadowing normally occurs at the start of a movie or a scene and serves to entice or prepare the audience.

fourth wall. The invisible, imaginary wall that separates the actors from the audience and the story from the real world. A character or narrator breaks the fourth wall when they directly address the audience, as the characters on *Modern Family* did on every show.

fps. Frames per second. Rate at which frames move through the camera or are played back during exhibition. In the United States, normally film runs at twenty-four fps and video at thirty fps.

frame. A single image that is the smallest unit of a shot.

frame rate. See **fps**.

Frankenbite. Also called *Frankenbyte.* Two or more dialogue lines or parts of lines from an interviewee pieced together to tell the story on a reality TV program.

freeze-frame. Also called *still frame.* A static "frozen" image that does not move, equivalent to a photo.

genre. Category of a film determined by its style, theme, plot, conventions, character types, and more. The main genres are action-adventure, comedy, documentary, drama, fantasy, film noir, horror, romance, sci-fi, and thriller.

helmer. See **showrunner**.

horror. Film genre designed to evoke nightmarish fears and dread with blood-chilling, spine-tingling happenings.

hybrid ending. Combination of closed ending and open ending that answers some questions but leaves others open. See also **closed ending** and **open ending**.

if/come. A type of contract that is most often offered to writers but can be offered to talent and crew. It stipulates that money will be paid only if the script is sold or the completed film makes a profit.

in medias res. Beginning a narrative in the middle of the plot or action; for example, starting a film with a chase scene.

intercut. (1) Cutting between two or more sequential scenes so that the scenes advance and complete together. See also **crosscut** and **parallel action**. (2) Cutting different images or sounds from different times and places within a scene. See also **montage scene**.

in the can. Derived from when shows were shot on film and the daily footage (film negative) was placed in cans (to be developed at the lab), "in the can" means the filming of a scene or an entire show is complete.

invisible editing. Editing that is so smooth that viewers become engrossed in the show and don't notice the individual cuts. The norm in editing.

irony. When the reality of a situation is opposite to what is stated, shown, believed, or ordinary, ratcheting up the conflict. For example, in the *Doc Martin* TV series, a brilliant surgeon must quit operating because he's afraid of blood.

jump cut. An edit in which objects or characters appear to jump because the shots are too similar. Technically, this is due to the camera angles of the two shots being less than thirty degrees apart.

jump the shark. To move a TV or movie series so far from its original premise that it loses credibility.

juxtaposition. How two shots edited next to each other impact each other; the sum of the cut is greater than the two shots in themselves.

key shot. See **matte shot**.

kill your darlings. Remove what doesn't work or belong, no matter how much you're attached to it.

lift. Remove and file a cut scene, section, or part of a scene during editing.

linear structure. Chronological story line composed of events unfolding as they happened in time.

locked cut. See **final cut**.

logline. Also called *one-liner*. A short—one line, preferably—high-concept summary of a screenplay used to pitch and sell it.

master shot. Shot that encompasses all the action in a scene from beginning to end. Although a master routinely starts framed close on a small object and can zoom and pan as needed to capture the action, it mostly stays wide to frame all the action.

match cut. Making an edit (cut) for continuity where the majority of the elements are duplicated (matched) from the first shot to the second shot. The elements to match are screen direction, eyeline, camera angle and framing, props, sound (wording, volume, or pacing), weather, wardrobe, hair, makeup, lighting, color, and action.

matte shot. Also known as *key shot.* Cutting a hole of any size or shape in a shot and placing another shot in the hole.

metaphor. A figure of speech composed of words, objects, or ideas that compares something to something else, such as the mysterious to the known or the abstract to the concrete or vice versa. Examples: "Life is like a box of chocolates," from *Forrest Gump,* and "You can put a cat in an oven, but that don't make it a biscuit," from *White Men Can't Jump.* Visual and thematic metaphors are evident in many a movie; the ones in *Avatar* include (1) the US military attacking the blue people of the planet Pandora, according to director James Cameron, is a metaphor for the US military attacking Iraq; (2) the Pandorans living harmoniously with nature and the military toppling their revered Tree of Souls can be seen as a metaphor for humankind's destruction of planet Earth.

mise-en-scène. The design of the setting and all its elements—actors, props, costumes, and so on—and how they are positioned and moved within a shot.

mismatch. A cut in which continuity is lost due to a difference between elements such as action, eyeline, camera framing, camera position, prop, wardrobe, or makeup. See also **continuity** and **match cut.**

montage scene. A succinct, self-contained sequence of images inserted to convey facts, feelings, or thoughts that usually functions as a transition in time or place. See also **action scene** and **dialogue scene.**

motivation. An editing caveat enjoining that each cut in a show advances its story, action, flow, and thought process.

MTV effect. A loose term for a type of filmmaking born with MTV that speeds up average shot lengths and infuses scenes with handheld camera movements and multiple everything—cuts, VFX, and story lines—while eliminating dialogue and letting music dominate the (sometimes thin) story.

narration. Also called *voice-over (VO).* Words spoken over the picture by an unseen character or narrator to describe an event or reveal a character's thoughts.

narrative transportation. Losing oneself in the world of story (film, podcast, literature, or other medium) and identifying with the character's goals and dilemmas.

New Wave. Theory of filmmaking initiated in 1951 by French film critics and filmmakers who decried Hollywood film style and promoted jump cuts, handheld camera, and the auteur theory while condemning artifice and traditional editing and emphasizing reality and cinema verité. See also **auteur theory** and **cinema verité.**

nonlinear structure. Asynchronous story time line not bound by the order in which events actually occurred.

obligatory scene. Scene that the drama or genre demands and the audience expects, such as a confrontation between the protagonist and the antagonist, a love scene in a romance, or a shoot-out in a Western.

offscreen. For visuals, an action, character, or object that is not seen in the shot. For sound, dialogue, sound effect, or music whose source is not seen in the shot.

offscreen space. An unseen area outside the frame that viewers are aware of due to an on-screen character(s) reacting to these hidden elements or characters.

one-liner. See **logline.**

one sheet. (1) A small movie poster, twenty-seven by forty-one inches, that advertises a film. (2) A one-page marketing advertisement for a product of any kind, letter size or larger.

on the nose. Dialogue, plot elements, sounds, or music that reflects exactly what a character is thinking or feeling and lack depth, subtlety, subtext, or nuance making for an uninteresting drama and unrealistic characters who don't act like real human beings.

open ending. Ambiguous conclusion that leaves unresolved questions, plots, or conflicts. See also **closed ending** and **hybrid ending.**

outtake. Camera take that is left out of the show.

pan. Shots in which the camera moves horizontally, left to right or vice versa.

parallel action. Intercut scene with two (or more) independent lines of action—characters, settings, or subjects—that do not interact directly and are unaware of each other. Scenes are independent of each other and rely on viewers to make the connection. See also **intercut.**

personification. Bestowing human characteristics on animals, objects, or natural phenomenon. Animation routinely personifies all manner of creatures (e.g., *SpongeBob SquarePants*) as do live action movies (e.g., Hal the computer in *2001: A Space Odyssey*).

phases of filmmaking:

> **green-lighting.** The first phase of a show, when it is formally approved and acquires financing. Once green-lit (or green-lighted), a film moves into the development phase. However, as with all phases of filmmaking, green-lighting commonly overlaps with other phases, specifically the development and preproduction phases.

> **development.** During this phase, the script (on fiction shows) or outline (on documentaries) is set, and director, producers, casting director, principal talent (actors, interviewees, experts) are hired.

> **preproduction.** Preparatory phase when script and finances are finalized, the rest of the talent and crew hired, locations and schedules locked, and storyboards, sets, wardrobe, and props created. On animated- and video effects (VFX)-driven shows, previsualization takes place in the editing room or VFX house to plan and prepare for the shoot.

> **production.** Also called *principal photography* or *the shoot*. This fourth phase encompasses the primary filming on set and location and creation of VFX.

> **postproduction.** Also called *editorial, editing,* or simply *post*. Fifth and final creative phase of filmmaking: all picture and sound editing take place,

music is composed, sound mixed, VFX finalized, and all other finishing work completed. Post produces the final show for viewing on tape, file, disk, and/or film.

distribution. Sixth and final phase, when the finished show goes to market (with a little or a lot of marketing!) and is delivered to its audience.

picture editor. See **editor.**

pitch. To present an idea for a film or TV series to those who can green-light (approve) the project, normally studio producers or execs.

plot. The chain of events in a story that make up its story line. See also **theme.**

plot twist. A sudden turn of events in a story that viewers didn't expect and that sends the film in a different direction.

point-of-view (POV) shot. A variation of a reverse shot, a POV shot corresponds exactly to *where* a character or person is looking; it is *what* they're seeing. In storytelling, POV can be subjective (from one character's POV) or omniscient (from an all-seeing and all-knowing observer). See also **reverse.**

postvisualization. On VFX-driven shows, as CGI and other VFX elements become available, the editor drops them into the edit for visualization, timing, and placement purposes. Similar to previsualization except that it occurs during postproduction. Sometimes shortened to *postvis* or *postviz*.

prequel. Movie (or book, TV show, play, video game) with a story that precedes a story that has previously been told in a movie (or book, etc.). An example is the original *Star Wars* movie, which was the fourth in the Star Wars series and eventually had three movie prequels. See also **sequel.**

previsualization. Also shortened to *previs* or *previz*. Determining camera moves, lighting, and so forth ahead of production. Often done on animation shows, heavy-duty VFX shows, 3D shows, and those requiring playback or other preshot or cut scenes for use during the shoot.

producer. Person responsible for overseeing and delivering the project from start to finish. It is common to have several producers who manage different aspects or phases of a show.

prologue. A stand-alone scene that precedes and sets the stage for the film's main story and appears before the main story starts; for example, the crawling text "A long time ago in a galaxy far, far away" that opens *Star Wars*. Most films do not have a prologue but jump right into the story.

protagonist. The main character (or characters, institution, or force), typically good but not always, who pursues the story's goals. See also **antagonist.**

reverse. (1) An angle shot from the exact opposite angle of the master shot action (2) A cut to the opposite (reverse) angle of any shot (over-the-shoulder, close-up, etc.). The cut can be from the *front* of a character to *behind* the character (or vice versa), or *from* a character (or characters) *to* the character (or characters) they're facing.

reverse motion. Playing a shot backward so that the filmed action takes place from end to beginning.

rhythm. The duration of shots and the number of shots in an edited sequence. The shots could be short and many or long and few. Rhythm is the pace and timing of the cuts and how a cut scene moves and breathes, akin to the rhythm in music. Rhythm can expand or contract time, altering the original filmed timing of the event.

romance. A comedy or drama film genre centered on love between characters that pursues the many forms and twists relationships can take: tragedy, infidelity, illness, and so on.

rough cut. The first edited version of a show. It's considered rough because it is missing sound editing and mixing as well as final visual effects, graphics, and narration.

scene. A series of shots or a single shot that shows a complete story event with a beginning, middle, and end. It ends with a change in time, location, narrator, character, or action. An example: Dorothy traveling to Oz via her house.

scene heading. Line in a screenplay at the head of each scene that defines its time and location. Specifically, a scene heading states if it's an interior (INT) or exterior (EXT) scene along with its location, time of day, and year (if time shifting). For example: INT. RIVERSIDE CHURCH – NIGHT or EXT. WAILING WALL – DAY – 70 CE.

scope. See **CinemaScope.**

screen. To show a cut—a work in progress—to a director, producer, client, or a trusted group of allies not associated with the project for feedback.

screenplay. Also called *script.* The film's story, containing its characters, dialogue, and settings, which is the blueprint for acting, shooting, and editing.

script. See **screenplay.**

sequel. A follow-on story (or book, TV show, play, video game) that continues the story in another movie or TV series (or book, etc.), such as *Paddington 2.* See also **prequel.**

sequence. A series of intercut scenes that compose one event, such as the opening sequence of *La La Land,* which shows commuters in a tie-up on a freeway getting out of their cars to dance, sing, and skateboard before returning to their vehicles and taking off for their day.

setting. The time and place of the film's story, including its time period, season, and culture.

SFX. Sound effects.

shooting. See **phases of filmmaking: production.**

shooting board. See **storyboard.**

shooting script. The final screenplay used to shoot the picture. It may specify camera moves and character actions and contain other cinematographic and directorial details as well as notes on props.

shots, takes, edits, and cuts:

    shot. Camera start to camera stop.

    take. A shot that starts (or ends) with a camera slate (clapstick) that labels the scene and take, such as 13-1, 26A-2.

edit. Also called *cut.* The joining together of two different shots or two parts of the same shot to put a show together.

cut. A series of edits. "Cut" and "edit" are used interchangeably: An edit can be made up of cuts, a cut can be made up of edits. The terms are used as both nouns and verbs, understandable in context.

showrunner. Also called *helmer.* The executive producer on a TV show who holds the creative vision and control over the entire series. The showrunner is in charge of the writer's room, may be the creator of the series and direct episodes, and usually is a writer on the series. See also **director** and **executive producer.**

slo mo. VFX in which the pace of the action is decreased from what occurred in real time in front of the camera. This decrease is accomplished during filming or editing. See also **speedup**.

slug line. Line in a film script that describes an important action or detail about a character, such as what they're seeing or how they're reacting.

smash cut. An unexpected, lightning-quick cut designed to jar the audience by zapping the action from one place, object, person, or image to another.

sound editor. Editor who cuts the show's sound: dialogue, music, and/or sound effects (SFX).

speedup. VFX in which the pace of the action is increased from what occurred in real time in front of the camera. This increase is accomplished during filming or editing. See also **slo mo**.

static shot. A shot in which the camera does not move. Any movement comes from the action taking place.

still frame. See **freeze-frame**.

stock character. A recognizable character with predictable actions: the alcoholic snob, the warmhearted grade school teacher, the cynical teenager.

stock situation. A recognizable plot, such as a gunslinger fleeing from the law or a student toiling day and night to pass a class.

storyboard. Also called *shooting board.* Drawings of frames that visually represent the shooting script to show how scenes will look and flow, shot by shot. A storyboard can contain camera information (movement, lens, framing), dialogue, and notes.

stylized. The opposite of natural or realistic, a film that overemphasizes traits or omits details to evince a look, a feeling, a theme, the inside of a character's mind. Examples: *The Grand Budapest Hotel, Brazil,* and *Bladerunner.*

subliminal cut. An edit of one to three frames which zips by so fast that the viewer is only subliminally (subconsciously) aware of it.

subtext. The unspoken, underlying meaning in a story that the writer injects and the audience may or may not notice. A screenwriter conveys subtext in action, dialogue, image, metaphor, or theme.

superimposition. Also shortened to *super.* An effect in which two or more shots are held on top of each other full screen.

symbolism. Giving meaning to something by showing something else, such as an animal, object, shape, music refrain, narrative style, setting, color, or character. Examples: the color blue routinely stands for loneliness or sorrow; a snake for treachery, such as in the Harry Potter movie series where Slytherin, the name of a dorm, connotes a snake.

sync. Align (synchronize) recorded picture with recorded sound so that they play together as shot and can be edited.

tag. A short, self-contained scene that appears after the commercial following the conclusion of a TV episode and resolves a minor plot or shows an ancillary outcome and often runs under end credits.

take. See **shots, takes, edits, and cuts**.

teaser. (1) In TV, a short opening scene designed to hook viewers. (2) In movies, a short promo of a work in progress created to secure funds or an audience.

tech noir. Modern-day film noir set in a dystopian future where technology is distrusted. Examples: the *Terminator* series and *Snowpiercer*. See also **film noir**.

theme. The idea or message of a story that can be a lesson or a moral. A film's theme raises a question, although it may not answer it. For instance, *When Harry Met Sally* centers around a rocky friendship that evolves into a relationship, but the theme is male-female relationships, asking, "Can women and men be close friends without being lovers?" See also **plot**.

tilt. Shot in which camera moves vertically.

tracking shot. A shot in which the camera follows the action by moving on a track (forward or backward) or tilting (moving vertically up or down) or panning (moving horizontally left or right).

transition. Shift from one scene or shot to another. Accomplished by a cut or any manner of visual or audio effects, such as a dissolve, wipe, or superimposition.

treatment. A summary of a screenplay written in narrative prose in present tense from beginning to end that succinctly (five to ten pages, normally) describes its key elements—story, plotlines, main scenes, characters—to sell the script.

trim. Shorten a scene during editing.

two-shot. A shot showing two characters, usually framed medium and including their faces.

VFX. Also called *EFX, FX,* or *F/X.* Visual effects such as fades, dissolves, wipes, or superimpositions.

VO. Voice-over. Narration that is voiced offscreen.

wipe. Transition effect in which the incoming shot replaces the outgoing shot by appearing to wipe (erase) it from the screen. Wipes are usually horizontal or vertical but can come from any corner or the interior of a shot.

Selected Bibliography

Akande, Zainab. "How to Measure Your Documentary's Impact and Make It Count." *IndieWire*, September 16, 2014. https://www.indiewire.com/features /craft/how-to-measure-your-documentarys-impact-make-it-count-22182/.

Allen, O. Wesley, Jr. *Determining the Form*. Minneapolis: Fortress Press, 2018.

———. *The Homiletic of All Believers: A Conversational Approach to Proclamation and Preaching*. Louisville, KY: Westminster John Knox Press, 2005.

Allen, O. Wesley, Jr., and Carrie La Ferle. *Preaching and the Thirty-Second Commercial: Lessons from Advertising for the Pulpit*. Louisville, KY: Westminster John Knox Press, 2021.

Bartesaghi, Simone. *The Director's Six Senses: An Innovative Approach to Developing Your Filmmaking Skills*. Studio City, CA: Michael Wiese Productions, 2016.

Boorstin, Jon. *Making Movies Work: Thinking like a Filmmaker*. Los Angeles: Silman-James Press, 1995.

Boyle, Alan. "Be Afraid. Be Very Afraid: IBM's Watson Makes AI Trailer about 'Morgan' AI Movie." *GeekWire,* August 31, 2016.

Britdoc.org/Impact. "Meet the Impact Producer." *The Impact Field Guide and Toolkit: From Art to Impact*. https://impactguide.org.

Cannon, Sarra. "How to Plan and Write a Series: The Different Types of Series." *Heart Breathings* (blog), July 9, 2020. https://heartbreathings.com/ the-different-types-of-series-how-to-plan-write-a-series-1/.

Cargal, Timothy B. *Hearing a Film, Seeing a Sermon: Preaching and Popular Movies*. Louisville, KY: Westminster John Knox Press, 2007.

Chandler, Gael. *Cut by Cut: Editing Your Film or Video*. 2nd ed. Studio City, CA: Michael Wiese Productions, 2012.

———. *Editing for Directors: A Guide for Creative Collaboration*. Studio City, CA: Michael Wiese Productions, 2021.

———. *Film Editing: Great Cuts Every Filmmaker and Movie Lover Should Know*. Studio City, CA: Michael Wiese Productions, 2009.

Cherry, Brigid. "Refusing to Refuse to Look." In *Identifying Hollywood's Audiences: Cultural Identity and the Movies,* edited by Melvyn Stokes and Richard Maltby. London: British Film Institute, 1999.

Cutting, James, Jordan DeLong, and Christine Nothelfer. "Attention and the Evolution of Hollywood Film." *Psychological Science Online*, February 5, 2010.

Dawn, Randee. "Screenwriters on Nailing That All-Important Opening Scene." *Variety*, January 3, 2020. https://variety.com/2020/film/awards/screenwriters -first-scene-lena-waithe-greta-gerwig-noah-baumbach-1203456297.

DeMos, Jackson. "Research Study Finds That a Film Can Have a Measurable Impact on Audience Behavior." USC Annenberg School for Communication and Journalism. Updated May 3, 2023. https://annenberg.usc.edu/news/centers /research-study-finds-film-can-have-measurable-impact-audience-behavior.

Engel, Joel. *Oscar-Winning Screenwriters on Screenwriting*. New York: Hyperion, 2002.

Fadiman, Dorothy, and Tony Levelle. *Producing with Passion: Making Films That Change the World*. Studio City, CA: Michael Wiese Productions, 2008.

Frost, Jacqueline B. *Cinematography for Directors: A Guide for Creative Collaborations*. 2nd ed. Studio City, CA: Michael Wiese Productions, 2020.

Gurskis, Dan. *The Short Screenplay: Your Short Film from Concept to Production*. Aspiring Filmmaker's Library, 2011, Kindle.

Hannan, Shauna K. *The Peoples' Sermon: Preaching as a Ministry of the Whole Congregation*. Working Preacher Books. Minneapolis: Fortress Press, 2021.

———. "Impact Teams." Part 2 of "What Preachers Can Learn from Filmmakers." *Teaching with Digital Media* (blog), February 17, 2020. Wabash Center for Teaching and Learning in Theology and Religion. https://www.wabashcenter .wabash.edu/2020/02what-preachers-can-learn-from-filmmakers-part -2-of-4-impact-teams/.

———. *Teaching with Digital Media*. Crawfordsville, IN: Wabash Center for Teaching and Learning in Theology and Religion, 2020.

Heimann, Katrin S., Sebo Uithol, Marta Calbi, Maria A. Umiltà, Michele Guerra, and Vittorio Gallese. "'Cuts in Action': A High-Density EEG Study Investigating the Neural Correlates of Different Editing Techniques in Film." *Cognitive Science* 41 (2017): 1555–88.

Hirsch, Paul. *A Long Time Ago in a Cutting Room Far, Far Away. . . .* Chicago: *Chicago Review Press*, 2019.

Johnston, Robert K., Craig Detweiler, and Kutter Callaway. *Deep Focus: Film and Theology in Dialogue*. Grand Rapids: Baker, 2019.

Kernan, Lisa. *Coming Attractions: Reading American Movie Trailers*. Austin: University of Texas Press, 2004.

Kim-Cragg, HyeRan. *Postcolonial Preaching: Creating a Ripple Effect*. Lanham, MD: Lexington Books, 2021.

Larsen, Josh. *Fear Not! A Christian Appreciation of Horror Movies*. Eugene, OR: Cascade Books, 2023.

Lowry, Eugene. *The Homiletical Beat: Why All Sermons Are Narrative*. Nashville: Abingdon Press, 2012.

———. *The Homiletical Plot: The Sermon as Narrative Art Form*. Louisville, KY: Westminster John Knox Press, 2000.

Lyden, John C. *Film as Religion: Myths, Morals, and Rituals*. 2nd ed. New York: New York University Press, 2019.

Magliano, Joseph P., and Jeffrey M. Zacks. "The Impact of Continuity Editing in Narrative Film on Event Segmentation." *Cognitive Science* 35 (2011).

McFee, Marcia. *Think like a Filmmaker: Sensory-Rich Worship Design for Unforgettable Messages.* Truckee, CA: Tokay Press, 2016.

McClure, John. *The Roundtable Pulpit: Where Leadership and Preaching Meet.* Nashville: Abingdon, 1995.

McKenzie, Alyce M. *Making a Scene in the Pulpit: Vivid Preaching for Visual Listeners.* Louisville, KY: Westminster John Knox Press, 2018.

McKenzie, Alyce M., and Owen Hanley Lynch. *Humor Us! Preaching and the Power of the Comic Spirit.* Louisville, KY: Westminster John Knox Press, 2023.

Mercurio, Jim. *The Craft of Scene Writing: Beat by Beat to a Better Script.* Fresno, CA: Quill Driver Books, 2019.

Murch, Walter. *In the Blink of an Eye: A Perspective on Film Editing.* 2nd ed. Los Angeles: Silman-James Press, 2001.

Nash, Jamie. *Save the Cat! Beat Sheet Workbook: How Writers Turn Ideas into Stories.* Los Angeles: Save the Cat! Press, 2022.

Ntim, Zac. "Steven Spielberg on Ending 'Schindler's List' with Cemetery Scene." *Deadline*, January 29, 2023. https://deadline.com/2023/01/steven-spielberg -schindlers-list-cemetery-scene-ending.

Pahl, Jon. *Empire of Sacrifice: The Religious Origins of American Violence.* New York: New York University Press, 2010.

Renninger, Bryce J. "How Do We Measure the Impact of Documentaries? Data from the Puma Impact Award Nominees." *IndieWire*, November 12, 2013. https://www.indiewire.com/features/craft/how-do-we-measure-the-impact-of -documentaries-data-from-the-puma-impact-award-nominees-33061/.

Romanowski, William D. *Cinematic Faith: A Christian Perspective on Movies and Meaning.* Grand Rapids: Baker Academic, 2019.

Rose, Lucy Atkinson. *Sharing the Word: Preaching in the Roundtable Church.* Louisville, KY: Westminster John Knox Press, 1997.

Rosen, Judy. "Sunday Night Lights: How America's Most Spectacular TV Show Gets Made," *New York Times Magazine*, December 2, 2023, https://www.nytimes .com/2023/12/02/magazine/sunday-night-football.html.

Rosenbloom, Ralph, and Robert Karen. *When the Shooting Stops . . . the Cutting Begins: A Film Editor's Story.* New York: Viking Press, 1979.

Rydall, Derek. *There's No Business Like Soul Business: A Spiritual Path to Enlightened Screenwriting, Filmmaking, and Performing Arts.* Studio City, CA: Michael Wiese, 2007.

Sandlin, Jennifer. "Evangelicals Rail against Barbie, Demand Americans Not Take Children to See Film." *boingboing*, July 20, 2023. https://boingboing.net /2023/07/20/evangelicals-rail-against-barbie-demand-americans-not-take-children -to-see-film.html.

Schwartz, Don. *Telling Their Own Stories: Conversations with Documentary Filmmakers.* Berkeley, CA: Don Schwartz, 2013.

Sharma, Versha, and Hanna Sender. "Hollywood Movies with Strong Female Roles Make More Money." Vocativ, January 2, 2014. Cited in Alanna Vagianos, "This Graph Proves That Everyone Loses When Hollywood Is Sexist," *Huffington Post*, January 3, 2014. https://www.huffpost.com/entry/hollywood-sexist-bechdel -test-vocativ_n_4536277.

Singer, Michael. *A Cut Above: 50 Film Directors Talk about Their Craft.* Los Angeles: Lone Eagle Publishing, 1998.

Tarkovsky, Andrei. *Sculpting in Time.* Austin: University of Texas Press, 1985.

Thomson, David. *How to Watch a Movie.* New York: Vintage Books, 2017.

Tibbs, Ros. "Spielberg Explains the Powerful Ending of 'Schindler's List.'" *Far Out*, February 1, 2023. https://faroutmagazine.co.uk/steven-spielberg-explains-ending -schindlers-list/.

Travis, Sarah. *Decolonizing Preaching: The Pulpit as Postcolonial Space.* Eugene, OR: Wipf & Stock, 2014.

Trible, Phyllis. *Texts of Terror: Literary-Feminist Readings of Biblical Narratives.* Philadelphia: Fortress Press, 1984.

Troeger, Thomas. *Ten Strategies for Preaching in a Multimedia Culture.* Nashville: Abingdon, 1996.

Troeger, Thomas and H. Edward Everding Jr. *So That All Might Know: Preaching That Engages the Whole Congregation.* Nashville: Abingdon, 2008.

Truby, John. *The Anatomy of Genres: How Story Forms Explain the Way the World Works.* New York: Picador, 2022.

Truffaut, Francois. *Hitchcock.* New York: Simon & Schuster, 1966.

Turner, William C., Jr. "The Musicality of Black Preaching." In *Performance in Preaching: Bringing the Sermon to Life,* edited by Jana Childers and Clayton Schmidt. Grand Rapids: Baker, 2008.

Vedantam, Shankar, Laura Kwerel, and Tara Boyle. "Why We Love Surprises: The Psychology of Plot Twists." *Hidden Brain: A Conversation about Life's Unseen Patterns,* NPR, December 23, 2019. https://www.npr.org/series/423302056 /hidden-brain.

Vogler, Christopher. *The Writer's Journey: Mythic Structure for Writers.* Studio City, CA: Michael Wiese Productions, 2020.

Van Sijll, Jennifer. *Cinematic Storytelling: The 100 Most Powerful Film Conventions Every Filmmaker Must Know.* Studio City, CA: Michael Wiese Productions, 2005.

Weintraub, Bernard. "Hollywood's Kindest Cuts: Invisible Film Editors Start to Emerge from Director's Shadow." *New York Times,* August 20, 1998.

Wilkinson, Alissa. "In the Beginning, There Was Barbie: Turns Out Greta Gerwig's Barbie Movie Is a Biblical Metaphor after All." *Vox,* July 20, 2023. www. vox.com/culture/23800753/barbie-review-bible-eden.

Yamasaki, Gary. *Insights from Filmmaking for Analyzing Biblical Narrative.* Minneapolis: Fortress Press, 2016.

Index

Printed in the USA
CPSIA information can be obtained
at www.ICGtesting.com
CBHW030903251024
16365CB00014B/94